C000157401

Out of the Inkwell

Out of the Inkwell

MAX FLEISCHER AND THE ANIMATION REVOLUTION

Richard Fleischer

With a Foreword by Leonard Maltin

THE UNIVERSITY PRESS OF KENTUCKY

Publication of this volume was made possible in part by a grant
from the National Endowment for the Humanities.

Copyright © 2005 by Richard Fleischer
Paperback edition 2011

The University Press of Kentucky
Scholarly publisher for the Commonwealth,
serving Bellarmine University, Berea College, Centre College of Kentucky,
Eastern Kentucky University, The Filson Historical Society, Georgetown College,
Kentucky Historical Society, Kentucky State University, Morehead State University,
Murray State University, Northern Kentucky University, Transylvania University,
University of Kentucky, University of Louisville, and Western Kentucky University.
All rights reserved.

Editorial and Sales Offices: The University Press of Kentucky
663 South Limestone Street, Lexington, Kentucky 40508-4008
www.kentuckypress.com

 Betty Boop Artwork: ©2005 King Features Syndicate, Inc./Fleischer Studios, Inc.
™Hearst Holdings, Inc./Fleischer Studios, Inc.

The Library of Congress has cataloged the hardcover edition as follows:
Fleischer, Richard.
   Out of the inkwell : Max Fleischer and the animation revolution / Richard Fleischer ; with a
foreword by Leonard Maltin.
      p. cm.
   Includes bibliographical references and index.
   ISBN 0-8131-2355-0 (hardcover : alk. paper)
   1. Fleischer, Max, 1883-1972. 2. Animators—United States—Biography. I. Title.   NC1766.
U52F5834   2005
   791.43'34'092—dc22
   ISBN 978-0-8131-3464-2 (pbk. : alk. paper)

This book is printed on acid-free paper meeting the requirements of the American National
Standard for Permanence in Paper for Printed Library Materials.

Manufactured in the United States of America.
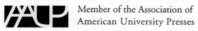 Member of the Association of
American University Presses

O! it is excellent
To have a giant's strength, but it is tyrannous
To use it like a giant
　　　　—Shakespeare, *Measure for Measure*

Contents

Illustrations follow page 82

Foreword

Leonard Maltin

Max Fleischer is animation's unsung hero. If Walt Disney is the most celebrated and chronicled producer in the history of the medium, Fleischer is his polar opposite.

Animation fans love his work and revere his cartoons' unique personality and technical achievements. Watching the innovative *Out of the Inkwell* shorts from the 1910s and 1920s is as joyful and exciting today as it must have been when they were new. Those shorts also give us a glimpse of Max, as he appears on-screen opposite Ko-Ko the Clown. The *Popeye* cartoons continue to delight audiences lucky enough to see them after nearly seventy years. Betty Boop has become a pop culture icon in recent years, but her starring films of the 1930s seem just as contemporary as she does, retaining every bit of their charm and spunk. The *Superman* cartoons of the early 1940s are the most impressive of all in terms of sophisticated dramatic staging and special effects.

Fleischer's career has been chronicled by a handful of animation scholars. We know about his invention of the Rotoscope, which enabled him to trace live-action movements, and his early experiments with sound. We know how he was pressured to compete with Walt Disney in the perilous production of feature-length cartoons. But we still don't know very much about the man himself. Thank goodness his son Richard decided to write a full-fledged biography.

The story is told from a highly personal point of view, as it should be, but at the same time it fills many gaps in our knowledge of Max Fleischer's career, with its triumphs, twists, turns, and setbacks.

I learned a great deal about Max's family, his aspirations and disappointments, and his poignant final years, and I came away with a renewed sense of appreciation for what he accomplished, often against tremendous odds.

Max Fleischer has long been a hero to anyone who loves animated cartoons. Now, thanks to his son, we can get to know the very human figure behind all those wonderful films.

Preface and Acknowledgments

The phone in my office in Los Angeles got out no more than two rings before I answered. "Hello," I squeaked, pretending to be wide awake. The phone responded with: "Can you tell me if . . ." "MAX WILK," I shouted. "It's MAX WILK!" "How did you know that?" Wilk asked in genuine astonishment. "That's easy," I replied. "All you have to do is listen to that drawling 'New York–ese' for a couple of minutes. You'll never wash it out of your ears."

To make sense out of this conversation, you have to know that Max Wilk and I attended the Yale School of Drama together for three years. We became good, lifelong friends. Sometimes years go by with no contact, but when we meet again, we always pick up where we left off—with lots of laughs since Max Wilk became, and remains, one of this country's most prolific and wittiest writers, with many best sellers to his name.

Anyhow, Wilk jumped into the reason for his call. He'd heard through the grapevine that I had written a book about my father, and he'd love to get a glimpse. It didn't take much urging. An express package was on its way that evening. A day or two later Wilk phoned again. He'd like to have some more friends read it too.

Another couple of days went by, and I received calls from some well-connected friends of Wilk's. A few more weeks went by, and Larry Mirisch, a young man whom I've known since he was a boy and who is now one of the most successful agents in Hollywood, contacted me. Could he send a manuscript to a person I'd never met?

Finally, I found myself talking on the phone about my book to a lady named Leila Salisbury, the marketing manager of the University Press of Kentucky, and her film acquisition assistant, John Hussey. And after that it was a hop, skip, and jump to contract signing.

I use this long-winded summary to demonstrate how dedicated people can move things right along, so a loud and long thank-you for your dedication to this book to Max Wilk, Stanley Handman (a partner and whiz of a lawyer), Larry Mirisch, and Sarah Stanick (assistant extraordinaire who knows where everything is and how to use it); as well as Leila Salisbury, John Hussey, Ira Skutch (for his moral support), Ann Berns (for her cheerful encouragement), and Anthony Slide (without whom this book would not have found its publisher); and, finally, Mark Fleischer (son and lawyer extraordinaire), Bruce Fleischer and Jane Reid (lawyers and son and daughter extraordinaire), my wife, Mickey (for urging me on), and, of course, the one and only Max Fleischer.

Out of the Inkwell

1

They say that it's difficult being a famous man's son, that you live in his shadow, that comparisons with him are always odious. Well, I grew up as a famous man's son, and I didn't find it difficult at all. In fact, it was great. My father, Max Fleischer, was a famous man and a celebrity for my entire childhood and young adulthood, and far from living unhappily in his shadow, I thoroughly enjoyed basking in the reflected glow of his limelight. When I was a kid, just mentioning to a theater manager that I was Max Fleischer's son got me into the movie for free. When I traveled in Europe with my mother and sister, once the people at passport control got a look at her name they would say to my mother: "Madame, are you the wife of Max Fleischer?" When she would answer that she was, the stony faces would break out in surprised smiles, and they would graciously wave us through, usually saying something like: "Welcome to our country, and please tell your husband how much we love his wonderful cartoons."

Believe me, that kind of treatment did great things for this teenager's ego. And later in life the name helped open professional doors for me. Once inside, I was on my own, but the name got me in there.

My father had no such advantage when, in 1887, at the age of four, he stepped off the SS *Rotterdam* and through the doors of Ellis Island with his mother, Amelia, and his year-older brother, Charlie. His father, William, had come over the previous year, and he was no celebrity. He was an immigrant Austrian tailor, one of the huddled masses yearning to be free. A small, thin, aesthetic-looking man, he seemed more like an artist or a musician, which he also was (he was a violinist), than a plebeian tailor.

After a series of moves, William and Amelia settled down in the Brownsville section of Brooklyn, New York—a countrified district of small houses with small plots of land—at 98 Powell Street, where they eventually produced four more children, Joe, Louis, Dave, and Ethel. William Fleischer opened a tailor shop in Manhattan and after several moves ended up at 69 West Forty-sixth Street, the present site of Rockefeller Center.

But William Fleischer was no ordinary tailor, and his shop wasn't ordinary either. He specialized solely in women's riding habits, and in order to fit his clients he installed a stuffed horse in the shop. It was probably the only tailor shop in New York with a stuffed horse, but with a sidesaddle in place the ladies knew they'd be fitted properly. Word of his skill must have traveled quickly because soon he numbered among his clients the Rockefellers, the Vanderbilts, the Astors, and all the other swells of Manhattan.

William also had his own claim to fame: besides being a

tailor he was also an inventor. His shop was fairly close to a police station, and some of the cops used to stop by for an occasional chat. They all seemed to have the same general complaint: whenever they polished their metal uniform buttons, it was almost impossible not to stain the uniform material as well. William solved that problem by inventing the removable button. He also invented a device for accurately marking the height of a hemline by attaching a movable rubber bulb filled with chalk powder to an upright wooden yardstick. Adjust the rubber bulb to the desired height on the stick, give it a squeeze, and, presto, a spurt of chalk would mark the exact height off the floor the hem should be and would continue to do so as the stick with its bulb was moved around the skirt.

It wasn't too long after the Fleischers moved to Powell Street that another new family took up residence about a block away. They were the Goldsteins, Harris and Anna, who, a few years back, had emigrated from London, where they had run a music hall/restaurant of sorts, bringing with them their four beautiful daughters, Annie, Essie, Debbie, and Bessie.

Harris Goldstein was a bald-headed gent with a fringe of fiery red hair to match his temper. His body resembled a thick, sturdy oak. In our family he was always referred to as "the Tree." For some mysterious reason, when Harris and Anna left England for the United States, the family name was Spadder, but by the time they exited Ellis Island, it had somehow become Goldstein. At that time, Ellis Island was overflowing with immigrants, and the immigration officers were very impatient. They were particularly impatient with those who were having language difficulties, which was certainly the case with Harris Spadder, whose mother tongue was Russian. How true it is, I don't know, but I've heard that immigration officers would ask an immigrant his name and that, if the immigrant didn't understand the question and looked Jewish, the officer would say: "Okay, your name is Goldstein [or Levy, or whatever]. Next!" Maybe that's what happened to the name Spadder.

Harris's English—acquired during his stay in London—was a source of amusement in the neighborhood. Somehow he had picked up some Elizabethan English. He would greet a neighbor by saying something like: "Methinks it's going to raining today."

The only Fleischer boys old enough to show any interest in the Goldstein girls were Charlie and Max, who set about courting them by showing off their skills at trick bicycle riding. They'd ride back and forth in front of the Goldstein house with Charlie peddling the bike and Max standing on his head on the handlebars, or standing on one foot on Charlie's shoulder, or doing whatever it would take to get the girls' attention. After weeks of risking his body parts with daredevil stunts, the antics paid off, not for Charlie, but certainly for Max, who finally took a header while doing an ill-advised handstand on the bike's rear fender. This finally got Essie's attention. She ran off the porch, lifted his head from the clinging dirt, and was greeted with a bloodied, but grinning, face. Max found himself staring into startlingly blue eyes set in a mischievous, pretty face topped with a jumble of auburn hair. The twelve-year-old Max and the twelve-year-old Essie became inseparable companions.

MaxandEssie. It became like a single word in the neighborhood. They were always together. They went to the same school, were in the same grade. He carried her books to and from her home. When he turned thirteen, Essie attended his bar mitzvah.

It was a long, slow courtship. By modern teenage standards, it moved along at the speed of a glacier, and Max and Essie kept to the rules and decorum of the times. Chaperoning was de rigueur. Being alone together in a room was definitely out. In fact, not only did they have to sit apart; they had to sit across the room from each other. But they had a secret weapon. There was a young neighborhood girl named Fanny who was deaf and dumb. To their credit, they had made a friend of her and had set about having her teach them sign language. They became quite adept at signing and got a huge kick out of sitting across the room from each other and signing *I love you* when no one was looking.

By the time Max was fourteen and ready to enter high school, something became increasingly apparent to him: he could draw. He didn't just love drawing; he was consumed by it. No matter what it took, he decided, he was going to be an artist. But he still had to reckon with his general education. Why he chose the Mechanics' and Tradesmen's Evening High School isn't clear. Perhaps he thought that a mechanic's education might be a handy fallback if his art plans didn't pan out. Perhaps he loved machinery and wanted to learn mechanical drawing. But why a night school? There is no explanation in any of his papers, memoirs, autobiographies, or biographies. The likeliest conjecture is that he had found a day job that would enable him to save enough money to further his plans for becoming an artist. And further his plans he did, in a most methodical, logical, determined, and quality-driven manner.

He finished his year at Mechanics' and Tradesmen's in 1897. The years 1898 and 1899 found him enrolled in the prestigious Art Students' League, where he studied under George B. Bridgman. The year 1900 found him at the Cooper Union Institute of Art, where he learned freehand drawing. Step by invaluable step he seemed to have had celestial guidance in making precisely the right decisions that would eventually take him to what seems now like an inevitable goal.

The romance with Essie, meanwhile, had been proceeding at its leisurely pace, but then something happened that would have destroyed most relationships. The Fleischer family moved to Manhattan. Brooklyn, in 1900, was a long way from Manhattan. Other than taking a ferry, the only way across the East River was the newly built Brooklyn Bridge. Henry Ford was still about ten years from populating the world with fast transportation. Horse-drawn trolleys were the thing—and, of course, the bicycle. But you would have to be in marathon shape to bicycle from Manhattan to Brooklyn. With the Fleischers now ensconced at 211 East Fifty-seventh Street, you would expect the romance to wither. It didn't.

Since telephones were still a rarity (there were just over a million in the entire country) and far too expensive for the average household, letter writing was almost the only mode of communication. Max and Essie kept up a constant flow of letters. A few of Max's, dated 1900 and 1901, still survive, offering a fascinating and charming insight into the art of courtship of the period. These are not quite love letters—mostly they discuss social events and the weather. But someplace in each he always drew a picture of two hearts pierced by an arrow, next to which he printed "Trade Mark." Every letter was signed with his full name, Max Fleischer, followed by his entire return address. The closest thing to passion in the letters in my possession is a note written in a margin that states: "I have enclosed 1,000,000,000 kisses."

One letter, in my opinion, has more than ordinary interest since it clearly foretells the future career of Max Fleischer. It seems that some mutual friends, a brother and sister named Lipp, had done some mischief by telling Essie that Max had met another girl in New York. When he heard about this, Max wrote Essie, vigorously denying this dastardly lie, and going on to say that if ever he gets hold of Lipp and his sister he'll "hit them a punch that will knock them cross-eyed so that when they cry, the tears will run down the back of their necks." If that isn't an animated cartoon image, then I don't know what is.

In the 1900 census, Max lists his age as seventeen and his occupation as artist. The occupation part was more ambition than fact since Max, as talented, well trained, and prepared as he was, had yet to find employment in his chosen profession. But that was soon to change.

The *Brooklyn Daily Eagle* was one of the most respected journals in the country. Because of its comic strips and editorial cartoons, to which he was fanatically devoted, it was the only newspaper that Max, a former Brooklynite, knew anything about. One day, he biked his way across the Brooklyn Bridge, found the *Eagle*'s offices, somehow or other got to meet Herbert S. Ardell, the manager of the Art Department, and made him a proposition. Max offered to pay the *Eagle* two dollars a week just to let him sit in the Art Department and watch the artists work. Recognizing talent when he saw it, Ardell made a counteroffer: the *Eagle* would pay Max two dollars a week to deliver papers from a horse-drawn wagon and be the Art Department's errand boy. Max leaped at the offer. He knew that once he got his foot in that door, the rest of him would soon follow.

No errand boy he. Ardell had opened the door to a whirlwind of unfettered talent. In no time at all Max became a copyboy and then trained as a photograph retoucher. Soon thereafter he was introduced to the art of news photography, learning the uses of lenses, optics, chemistry, composition, and photoengraving, and became the staff photographer.

2 Two years after joining the *Brooklyn Daily Eagle*, Max Fleischer was probably the youngest major-newspaper staff cartoonist in the country. Not only was he drawing editorial cartoons for the paper, but he had two regular comic strips of his own, *Algy* and *E. K. Sposher, the Camera Fiend*. Almost all his work is signed "Mack." *Algy* was the earlier of the two strips and, not surprisingly, seems influenced by the Brownsville environment: unpaved, muddy streets; wooden picket fences; and tough street gangs. It was, after all, the streets of Brownsville that later gave birth to the Mafia banker Meyer Lansky and Jacob "Gurrah" Shapiro, of Murder, Inc., fame. No wonder all the characters in Max's strip spoke in "dees, dem, and does" terms. Algy himself was a sort of numbskull, but romantic, loser, trying in vain to attract the attention of a bland young girl named May McGinnis. Algy's well-laid plans are always undone by Swipsey, a tough, young gang leader, and end with Algy's humiliation. In a strip

titled *Algy as Sir Walter Raleigh, Jr.,* Algy finds May unable to cross a street because of a large mud puddle. He immediately throws his jacket over the puddle, saying: "Yer kin use me coat fer er mat." May graciously says to herself: "Aint he de kind chump." Unfortunately, the coat isn't long enough to reach across the whole puddle. Along comes Swipsey, who fills in the gap with his own jacket. May crosses the puddle, but when Algy goes after her and steps on Swipsey's coat, Swipsey jerks it away, saying: "Git yer muddy hoofs off'n me coat." Algy lands on his face in the mud.

E. K. Sposher, the Camera Fiend is a great improvement in style and content. The character of Sposher is drawn with grace and is a classier gent all around. Tall, balding, well dressed, and living in upper-class surroundings, he is a fool nonetheless. As the strip announces, he is a camera nut and always appears equipped with a bellows camera with a frosted glass back and a tall, rickety tripod. In one strip, he decides to take a picture of himself by photographing his reflected image in a full-length mirror. The problem that he confronts is that his image appears upside down in the frosted glass in the back of the camera. His solution is to turn the camera upside down on the floor, with the tripod sticking straight up in the air, then standing on his head to look through the lens. When he reaches for the rubber air bulb that operates the camera shutter, he loses his balance, and he and the camera fall over, smashing the mirror.

Max spent four creative, priceless years at the *Eagle,* learning, growing, maturing. But it was his last year, 1904, that eventually proved to be the most important, the most fateful of his entire career. A new member joined the Art Department staff, not as a cartoonist, although he was one, but as a decorator, someone who drew decorations around the framework of the pictures in the Sunday paper, as was the style in those days. He was a bit older than Max, had been around, and was an experienced professional. As the newest members of the Art Department, he and Max gravitated toward each other and became friends. This newcomer—John Randolph Bray—was destined to become one of the most important figures in the history of animated cartoons. He would, one day, hold my father's career in his hands.

In the meantime, Max was getting restless at the *Eagle*. Having started there at two dollars a week, four years later he wasn't pulling down very much more. It was time to move on to a more lucrative job. So, late in 1905, he left the *Eagle* and went to work as an engraver at the Electro-Light Engraving Company in Boston.

Besides earning more money in his new job, Max picked up new skills like layout, design, lettering, reproduction, color work, and airbrush. All this expertise would prove invaluable for the career that lay ahead. Also, with the prospect of a better-paying job, he was able to marry Essie Goldstein. The ceremony took place at the American Star Hall in Brooklyn, at 6:00 P.M. on Christmas Eve, Sunday, December 24, 1905. One year later, almost to the day—December 28, to be exact—Essie gave birth to my sister, Ruth.

Max's span of job interest seems to have been limited to four years. In 1909, he pulled up stakes at Electro-Light and took his bride and his daughter to Syracuse, New York, where he had landed a job with the Crouse-Hinds Company, a manufacturer of turbines, generators, pumps, and machinery of various sorts. His job was to create the company's catalog, and it was a job he truly loved. Machinery fascinated him so much that, instead of illustrating the catalogs with photographs of the various products, he made etchings instead. They are so meticulously drawn that only by the closest observation, and by the artist's signature, can you detect that they are not photographs.

Eventually, Max came to the attention of a noted scientist, Waldemar Klaempffert, the editor in chief of *Popular Science Monthly* (later to become the science editor of the *New York Times*). Klaempffert obviously made Max an offer he in no way could or would refuse because, about a year after joining Crouse-Hinds, he was back in New York City working in the prestigious position of art editor of *Popular Science Monthly*.

3

If ever a job was tailor-made for anyone, the *Popular Science* job was it for Max. As Max writes in his 1939 unpublished autobiography: "I realized I was not only artistically inclined, but had a very keen and instinctive sense for mechanics. I liked them both. A strange combination. To me, machinery was an art also. I still see great art in machinery." So Max had his strange combination and reveled in it. True to form, he blossomed out, and, in addition to his other chores, it wasn't long before he was writing and illustrating technical articles on the latest inventions.

By the time he joined *Popular Science,* Max had become completely enamored of movies in general and of the primitive, jerky animated cartoons in particular. He was so fascinated with movies, in fact, that he thought it would be a good idea to open a movie theater in Brownsville, an area he was very familiar with and one that was growing like mad. Knowing that, because of the cost, a regular movie house would be out of the question, he approached his brother-in-law, Max Bertin, about helping to finance the opening of an outdoor movie theater, a popular venue for seeing films in the summertime. Bertin, the husband of Essie's sister Bessie, was a wholesale candy supplier and the only family member with a little loose change. Bertin liked the idea of being a movie impresario, and with the Fleischer brothers contributing their unique mechanical (Charlie), electrical (Joe), musical (Lou), and artistic (Max and Dave) talents, the whole venture could be done on the cheap.

The grand opening came, and so did the throngs. Throngs of mosquitoes, that is. Throngs, clouds, masses, hordes, a plague of mosquitoes. They ignored the movies but loved the audiences. However, they didn't come every night. On the nights they didn't come the rains came. To make matters worse, it poured rain most nights, and no amount of ladies' nights, when ladies got in free, or dish nights, when lucky ticketholders got free dishes, could make this doomed venture break even. Then came the coup de grâce. The following summer a hardtop Loews movie theater opened across the street. The outdoor movie venture was over, and its assets were distributed among the participants. There weren't many assets: secondhand collapsible wooden chairs; a battered upright piano; and a wood-sided, hand-cranked ancient Moy projector. Max ended up with the projector. He considered it a toy to tinker with.

Animated cartoons were nothing much to look at in 1915. They were called animated merely because they moved, and they did that in a crude, herky-jerky manner. In spite of that, audiences liked them. They were a curiosity. A pen-and-ink drawing that hiccuped and shuddered its erratic way around the screen, but it moved! Difficult and irritating to watch, these moving drawings had a magic about them. Waldemar Klaempffert had seen an animated cartoon about Theodore Roosevelt one evening at the movies and got so fed up with its rough technique that he actually became angry. He was still annoyed about that cartoon when he came to work the next morning. He called Max into his office and told him about his experience watching that cartoon. Then he said some prophetic words that would change Max's life: "Max, you're a bright young man. You're an artist, you understand mechanics, and machinery, and photography, and you've got a scientific mind. Surely you can come up with some idea, some way to make animated cartoons look better, smoother, more lifelike."

It was an idea that had occurred to Max before. But now, what with this gentle push from Klaempffert and his present work with inventions plus his love of machinery, his mind instinctively started to consider the idea of some mechanical help in the making of lifelike animated cartoons. The best way, he must have reasoned, to reproduce human body movement in a cartoon would be to copy it, in all its myriad detail, directly from a human in motion. The question was, How do you physically accomplish such a thing? Only some sort of machine might be able to do that. Suddenly, the answer was clear. There was such a machine, a machine whose sole purpose was to take a rapid succession of photographs of things in motion, pictures that would reveal the minutest detail of bodily movement, pictures that could then be traced in pen and ink. The machine was, of course, a motion picture camera. Finally, that strange combination, art and machinery, had come home to roost.

Max's concept was simplicity itself: take a piece of movie

film that has on it the image of a human being in motion and project this image, one frame at a time, onto a flat piece of glass. This projected image would, obviously, also be visible on the opposite side of the glass. All you would have to do is put a piece of paper over that image, trace its outline, then move on to the next frame. Once you had traced every frame of the projected image onto separate pieces of paper, you would then photograph each piece of paper. The process would be slow and tedious since it would take sixteen drawings to make just one second of film, but the final result would be a perfect copy of every movement, gesture, and expression of the original object.

As simple and as obvious as it was, no one had ever done it or even thought of it before. It was a completely original concept. Max immediately filed a patent application. He named his invention the Rotoscope.

But filing a patent application was one thing. Demonstrating that the theory really worked was another. Max started fooling around with the old Moy movie projector that he had inherited from the outdoor movie theater debacle to see whether it might somehow be adapted for use as a one-frame-at-a-time projector as well as a stop-frame camera. The more he experimented, the more excited he became. He needed someone to talk to, someone to share his excitement. He tried explaining it to Essie. My mother thought that it was just another one of his crazy ideas. The only one he knew who had some knowledge of moviemaking was Dave, his twenty-year-old younger brother, who was then working as a film editor at Pathé, a well-known movie-producing company. My father decided to tell Dave about the Rotoscope. He explained the system that he intended to use, and as he says in his autobiography: "Dave was fascinated by it. He couldn't sleep anymore." They were determined to get the Rotoscope built and running.

As usual, money was a problem. Once again, the Fleischer brothers volunteered their not inconsiderable talents. Joe was a master electrician. Charlie was a terrific mechanic. (He later invented that much-cursed amusement park machine the claw digger, the one that almost grabs the fancy prize buried in the cheap candy but usually ends up with a Tootsie Roll.) But, talented as they were, none of them had a dime to spare. My father had already used up every cent of his own savings, about $100, experimenting with the machine. And they couldn't go back to Max Bertin, the erstwhile movie-theater magnate. They needed someone to come to the rescue, someone with some money. And someone did appear: Essie. Out of her household expense allowance, my mother had somehow saved up about $150. She had other plans for that money, but she handed it over to Max, saying: "This is for your crazy idea."

There was still one hurdle left before the brothers could go to work. Where would they build and operate the Rotoscope? Max was still working at *Popular Science,* and the others were keeping their regular jobs as well. That meant that work on the Rotoscope would have to be done at night. What they needed was a place where they could work undisturbed during the night and no one would touch anything during the day. Once again Essie came through. She allowed them to use our living room— if they didn't upset it too much.

The first order of business was the construction of a rigid wooden framework that would hold the projector and the glass drawing board on which the images would be projected one frame at a time. The next was to photograph with a movie camera whatever it was that Max thought would be a good image to demonstrate his invention.

He decided on a clown because it would be universally understood in pantomime. Young Dave was cast to play this starring role. This was typecasting, Dave having actually been employed for a time as a clown at the famous Steeplechase Amusement Park in Coney Island. Max designed a baggy clown outfit with three large white buttons and a three-button conical hat and asked his mother to make it to fit Dave.

One fine day, with the old Moy projector now converted into a movie camera and loaded with 150 feet of thirty-five-millimeter negative film, the Fleischer brothers went up to the roof of Max's apartment house. There Max photographed a little over a minute's worth of Dave dancing, prancing, and pantomiming in front of the camera.

Max Fleischer had taken his first step into movie history.

Now, with the projector-cum-camera reconverted back into a projector, the work began. The task ahead was staggering—to understate it wildly. While the concept may have been simple, the execution was anything but. In those days, film ran through a projector at sixteen frames per second (today, twenty-four frames per second). The film that Max and his brothers had shot of Dave in the clown suit represented twenty-six hundred separate tracings that Max had to do. It sounds easy enough, but tracing the outline of a billowing clown suit requires great skill and immaculate, painstaking precision.

But this was only one part of the procedure. Once the drawings were completed, each and every one had to be photographed, one at a time. During his early experiments with the projector, Max had discovered that it had the wrong kind of shutter for one-frame-at-a-time photography. The only solution he could think of was to get rid of the shutter and use a lens cap instead. The challenge for Max was enormous. He had to expose the lens to the light by removing the lens cap from the camera for a fraction of a second, then recapping it. The critical part of the operation was that fraction of a second. It had to be precisely the same, with not the slightest variation whatsoever, each time the cap was removed and replaced. There was no margin for error. If Max wasn't dead-on with his timing each and every time, the whole project would be down the tubes.

With that comforting thought in mind, the Moy was loaded with unexposed negative film, and clown picture number 1 was put in place. Max removed and replaced the lens cap, and the camera crank was turned, advancing the second frame of the negative into position. One-sixteenth of a second's worth of work had now been immortalized on film.

Right from the beginning, the brothers would join Max in his living room each evening after work. Max would ask Essie not to disturb them, close the door, and they'd work from seven at night until three or four in the morning. In spite of the promise not to upset the room too much, it soon became a mess, with electric wires hanging from the chandeliers and motors, lathes, and tools all over the place. No one except the brothers—not even Essie—was ever allowed into this room at any time because the slightest disturbance could be ruinous to their work.

The work went ploddingly, uneventfully, until one evening. Here is my father's account of what happened: "We were getting pretty tired around 3:30 A.M. The household was asleep. I turned around and my elbow hit a bottle of ink and knocked it off the table and made a great big blot on the edge of the carpet. The blot was about as large as five fried eggs and we couldn't get it out. I knew right then that the experiment was over if the missus ever saw that. So quietly we tried to blot it up but it only looked worse. I said, 'Where do we go from here?' At 3:30 A.M. the three of us moved all the furniture out of that room, including a darn heavy upright piano, into the dining room, turned the rug around so that the spot came under the piano and we went on with our experiments for six months. Then we moved, and the ink spot was discovered. I got the same hell as though it had just happened."

Finally, as all jobs must, this one came to an end. Max and his brothers photographed the last clown picture, number 2,600. Max took the precious roll of exposed negative to a movie film laboratory to be developed. It represented a year's worth of work. For the final time, the poor old Moy was transformed back into a projector so that the developed film could finally be seen. As Max carried the processed film back home, he must also have carried quite a swarm of butterflies in his stomach. Were all the registrations in perfect alignment? Were the lens cap exposures consistent and accurate? Did the lab develop and print the film properly? Could a speck of dust, either in the camera or in the lab, have scratched the negative? There was plenty to worry about.

The crucial screening took place in the darkened living room of the apartment. The film was projected onto a two-foot-square piece of cardboard painted white. The projector light was switched on, the hand crank on the Moy was turned at the rate of sixteen frames per second, the five brothers held their collective breath, and there, on that tiny screen, they saw a cartoon that moved as no other cartoon had ever moved before, a cartoon clown that walked, ran, jumped, and danced with completely lifelike motion. The little clown was purely and utterly and delightfully human. It was alive. It was magic. Max's theory had been proved correct, and history had been made. The look of animated cartoons had been changed forever.

4

Brimming with pride and high hopes, Max couldn't wait until he could show his creation to a film distributor. This is the way my father remembered that event: "I took the film to a distributor and in the blink of the eye, it was run off. He said, 'That's very nice. What are you going to do with it?' I said, 'I don't know. I thought it was something, that's all.' He said, 'Could you make one of these every week?' I laughed. 'Why, no, it's a physical impossibility.' 'How long did it take you to make this thing?' he asked. 'It took about a year.' 'My dear fellow, go home and make something practical. If you had something we could offer for sale every week or every month, you'd have something, but once a year—Nix.'"

Max went home, depressed, but not dismayed. He knew he was on to something, something important. He began trying to think of shortcuts to get things done faster, of ways to bring down production time. He finally worked out a method that made it possible to produce about a hundred feet of film every fourth week. That made it a little more practical, but he still had a long way to go. What he needed was support from a big company so that he could continue his experiments. He felt that if he could get the right person to see the potential of what he had already accomplished, then he could revolutionize the field of animation.

So he kept on showing his film to anyone who would look at it, but no one seemed interested—until one afternoon he went to the offices of Paramount Pictures Distribution in Manhattan. He'd been everywhere else, and this was the last stop. He didn't even have an appointment; he was just waiting in the lobby outside the office of Paramount's president, Adolph Zukor, on the off chance that someone, anyone, would give him an interview. The door to Zukor's office opened, and, to his astonishment, out stepped his old buddy from the *Brooklyn Daily Eagle,* John Randolph Bray. *Serendipitous* is a poor and meager word to describe this meeting. *Earth-stopping* comes a little closer. Of all the chance meetings that Max could have had at this moment, one with J. R. Bray was the most fortuitous.

After leaving the *Eagle* about a year after Max, Bray went into the making of animated cartoons, and by this time, 1916, Bray Studios was by far the leader in the field. His *Colonel Heeza Liar* series was the most popular of his various productions. The reason he had been in Zukor's office was that he had a contract with Paramount for all the cartoons and short subjects of any kind that he could make. When Max told him about his small piece of film, Bray said: "You'd better come over to my studio and let me take a look at it." J. R. Bray now held Max's future in his hands.

Look at it he did—and found Max's cartoon funny and well animated. The really serendipitous part of the whole thing was that at his studio Bray had focused on finding ways to shorten production time and had, in fact, made tremendous strides in that direction. He was turning out cartoons so fast he seemed to be mass-producing them, and he was often referred to as "the Henry Ford of animation." He wasn't particularly pleased with that sobriquet because he would rather be known for the quality of his productions than for the speed with which they were made. Still, his biggest stride in speeding up production time was of historic proportions for cartoon animation. He and Earl Hurd, one of his employees, had developed and patented the Bray-Hurd animation process, which uses sheets of clear celluloid, or what are now known as *cels,* instead of sheets of paper. The savings in time are enormous. A background is drawn on one cel, and another cel, containing just the moving character, is placed on top of the first, superimposing the figure on the stationary background. To animate the character, you just keep replacing the top cel only. It is no longer necessary to redraw the background for every frame of film. Bray and Hurd patented this process so that no one else could use it without paying a licensing fee.

The accidental meeting of Max Fleischer and J. R. Bray seems almost preordained. There is Max with his revolutionary method of reproducing lifelike animation and thus making better movies but needing a way to speed up the animation process, and there is Bray with his revolutionary method of speeding up the animation process but needing a way to make better movies. These two revolutionaries were meant for each other.

Bray put Max under an exclusive contract and gave him the

assignment of producing one clown cartoon a month as part of his *Paramount Pictograph* series. Now that he had a cartoon series to make, Max needed a name for it. My father writes: "The title Out of the Inkwell was used for want of a better name. The pictures were done in pen and ink. In addition, there are so many things that can come out of an inkwell." (The clown didn't get the name Ko-Ko the Clown until much later.)

That wasn't the only thing that needed a name in 1916. I didn't come out of an inkwell, but on December 8 I needed a name too. For want of a better one, Max and Essie called me Richard.

So far, the portrait that I have drawn of my father has been pretty much a Rotoscope tracing, an outline that needs to be completed. In telling this early part of his story, I have mainly concentrated on his creativity, his mastery of technology, and his great determination to get where he wanted to go. That's because who he was and what he was like in his youth remain sketchy to me since there is no one still around who knew him then. Photographs show a slim, handsome young man with an impish smile, a short, straight nose, and a small mustache. I don't remember ever seeing him without that mustache. He couldn't remember being without it either. He used to say that he thought he must have been born with his mustache. I hope, later in this book, to fill in more fully the portrait of this remarkable man and to try to describe our very special relationship.

Max didn't get very far into production at Bray Studios when there was what could be considered a major interruption. On April 6, 1916, the United States entered World War I. As it happened, Bray Studios had a very good relationship with the U.S. Army. In fact, Bray had been making educational films for the government, most of which utilized some animation. Max had worked on several of those films, along with another Bray employee, Jack Leventhal, a brilliant mechanical draftsman. Because of these films, the military now wanted Bray to supply training films for the army, to be made at the School of Fire at Fort Sill, Oklahoma. Bray was happy to oblige and sent Max and Leventhal to do the job. They were working for the army but being paid by Bray. Being married, with two children, Max couldn't be drafted, but he was in the army anyhow. Bray himself never appeared at Fort Sill. It somehow smacks of the Civil War days when, if a drafted civilian didn't want to go, he could send a paid surrogate in his stead. Giving Bray his due, however, he never charged the government for the work and gave the films, covering over a hundred different subjects, to the army.

Max and Jack Leventhal spent the war years creating the first army training films ever made. They covered everything: contour-map reading; the operation of the Stokes mortar and the Lewis machine gun; even submarine mine laying. And all involved extensive animation. Max and Jack stayed with the assignment until the armistice in 1918. By that time, they had became devoted, lifelong friends.

With the war ended, Max and Jack returned to Bray Studios to continue their interrupted careers. Max also took along his brother Dave to help with the making of the *Out of the Inkwell* series and to continue to play the role of Ko-Ko the Clown. During the war, Dave had been able to hone his skills, particularly his great sense of timing, having been assigned by the War Department to work as a film editor at the Army Medical Museum in Washington, D.C.

Now back at Bray, Max and Dave faced having to turn out,

using the Bray-Hurd process, an *Inkwell* cartoon every month. This by itself would have been a challenge, but Max made the stakes a little higher by deciding that Ko-Ko alone was not enough. What Ko-Ko needed was someone to play against, and that someone was his creator, Max himself. The idea was to mix live action and animation. On-screen, Max, in live action, in a real setting, would dip his pen into an inkwell, then rapidly draw the image of Ko-Ko on the animation board in front of him. Ko-Ko would come alive, and there would be interaction between the clown and Max, with the clown climbing off the paper onto Max himself, then all over the room. Ko-Ko would create plenty of mischief until he was captured and put back into the inkwell with its cap firmly screwed on.

In April 1919, the first *Out of the Inkwell* cartoon was re-leased. It was an instantaneous, all-out hit. Audiences went mad about it. Critics gave it rave reviews. One reviewer described Ko-Ko as "a wonderful little figure that moves with the sinuous grace of an Oriental dancer." The *New York Times* critic wrote: "After a deluge of pen-and-ink 'comedies' in which the figures move with mechanical jerks with little or no wit to guide them, it is a treat to watch the smooth motion of Mr. Fleischer's figure and enjoy the cleverness that animates it." Another review read: "Mr. Fleischer's work, by its wit of conception and skill of ex-ecution, makes the general run of animated cartoons seem dull and crude." Max couldn't have written better reviews himself. All his work, effort, and anguish had paid off. He had accom-plished his ultimate goal—he really had changed the look of animated cartoons forever. He didn't realize it yet, but he had changed more than that.

Max's *Out of the Inkwell* series became such a worldwide hit that Bray made him a partner, a stockholder, and the studio's production manager. The cartoons were so popular that theaters started to advertise them on their marquees. In short, animated cartoons were finally finding their niche, and audiences were demanding to see more and more of them. Other animation studios were trying, unsuccessfully, to copy the Fleischer style. Up to that time, animated cartoons had always been considered more of a curiosity than anything else. Max and the Rotoscope had changed a curiosity into an industry.

The cartoons were marvels of invention, imagination, and charm and were also hilariously funny. No two cartoons ever started the same way. Ko-Ko makes his entrance in an almost infinite variety of brilliantly conceived ways: in one cartoon, a drop of ink drips off Max's pen onto a sheet of paper, the blot that it makes transforming itself into the figure of the clown; in another, a half-finished Ko-Ko grabs the pen and draws the rest of himself after Max is called away from the drawing board. The Fleischer trademark of surrealism and morphing is very much in evidence in all the cartoons. Even today these cartoons are just as funny and captivating as they ever were. Not too long ago I was invited to attend a silent movie festival in Pordenone, Italy. The organizers ran about sixteen of the *Inkwell* shorts. The audiences gave them rapturous attention, huge laughs, and thunderous applause. I couldn't help but think how gratified my father would have felt had he been there to see the loving reception given his eighty-year-old cartoons.

Even with the praise and the accolades that greeted Ko-Ko initially, however, Max felt that he could make his cartoons look even better. He wasn't completely satisfied that the Rotoscope permitted an animated figure to appear only in front of a stationary background, so, a few years later, he created a new invention, an improvement on the Rotoscope. He called it the Rotograph. The Rotograph allowed an animated figure to be superimposed not only over a stationary background but over a moving background as well. It also made combining cartoon animation with live action easier and the results more graceful.

5

Late in 1920, the Bray organization began to fall apart. It seems that, a year earlier, Bray had made a contract with the Goldwyn Company to produce and distribute all Bray's short films. Goldwyn capitalized the new venture to the tune of $1.5 million, a very substantial sum in those days. The Goldwyn-Bray goal was to release 156 reels of film a year. This was not just way beyond anything the Bray organization had ever produced before but way beyond anything it was actually capable of producing. By the end of the first year, it had released a total of twenty-eight reels, including some of the *Inkwell* cartoons. In a desperate move to make up the shortfall, Bray started buying for distribution films that were made by his biggest competitor, Hearst's International Film Service. The films didn't do well at all, and Goldwyn-Bray ended up owing a pile of money to the Hearst Corporation. By 1921, Bray and Goldwyn decided to call it quits. But there was further trouble afoot. The actors were getting restless, and many were starting to leave the company. The biggest embarrassment came when Earl Hurd departed and opened his own competing company. Because of the "new look" in cartoons, a lot of competition other than Earl Hurd's company was springing up.

In June 1921, Max and Jack Leventhal both left what seemed to be a sinking ship. Max formed Out of the Inkwell, Inc., and went into business for himself. It's not at all clear how he found the financing to do so. He had begun to build a name for himself, he had an impressive number of Ko-Ko shorts under his belt, and at that time the start-up financing that he would have required didn't amount to much, so perhaps he dipped into his own savings. Or perhaps Margaret Winkler, the film distributor with whom he signed, financed the new *Inkwell* series herself. It isn't an unreasonable assumption since a few years later she did just that for another animator, not on the basis of a tested and successful series like Max's, but merely on the basis of a screening of the pilot for a cartoon series. That animator's name was Walt Disney.

Wherever the financing came from, Max rented a small basement apartment in midtown Manhattan, furnished it with a few animation desks, a Rotograph, and some other basics, and, voilà, Out of the Inkwell, Inc., had a studio all its own. Dave brought in a friend who had worked with him in the army, Charlie Schettler, to do the animation photography. Charlie was the Fleischers' first employee and stayed with the company until it closed.

Because of the tremendous popularity of the *Inkwell* cartoons, animators wanted to work for the Fleischers. In no time at all the staff had grown to nine, and the studio had to move to larger quarters at 129 East Forty-fifth Street. But the company kept growing, and when the staff reached nineteen, it needed a lot more elbow room, so on November 30, 1923, it took over the entire sixth floor at 1600 Broadway. All this occurred within the space of just two years. The staff soon grew to 165, and additional space was taken on the seventh floor. The company, now called Out of the Inkwell Films, Inc., was by far the largest animation studio in New York.

The studio's expansion seemed to have happened with the suddenness of an automobile air-bag inflation. Animators were animating, inkers were inking, and about ninety other employees were working busily away, including relatives. Max found great use for his brothers. Usually, nepotism has a bad name, but in this case, better choices couldn't be found: Dave, a superb gag man, was the director of every cartoon ever made at the studio; Charlie, an inventor and top-notch mechanic, became the chief engineer and kept all the machinery running; Joe, a highly trained electrician, was head of the Electrical Department; and Lou, an accomplished musician, ran the Music Department. It was a perfect arrangement, and contrary to what usually happens when relatives work together, the brothers worked together harmoniously—initially at least.

Max's ambitions seemed to have expanded with the new workspace and the spreading, international popularity of his Ko-Ko the Clown. Max had started thinking about making films that were longer than a single reel when something came along that captured his imagination, along with that of the rest of the world: Einstein's theory of relativity. The press had given the theory plenty of attention, and the public showed enormous, but bewildered, curiosity about it. It was said that only about seven people in the world understood Einstein's theory, yet everyone was talking about it. For Max, with his scientific mind and background, the idea of making a serious film that would give the average person some idea of what it was all about was irresistible. So, in the same year as the move to 1600 Broadway, Max commenced work on *Einstein's Theory of Relativity* by enlisting the help of Professor Garrett P. Serviss, the highly esteemed science writer for the *New York American,* as well as other scientific mavens who were experts in Einstein's field of interest.

Max was really impressed with Serviss. Describing him in his unpublished autobiography, he writes: "During the production of Einstein's Theory of Relativity I was quite close to Prof. Serviss, an elderly man, somewhat hard of hearing but amazingly brilliant and with a mind that worked with the speed of light. His knowledge fascinated me as much as the work of making the picture. I realized that right near me was a mind which I could never attain." And this from a man who was frequently referred to as a genius himself. I include this quote because it reflects perfectly my father's self-effacing personality, his total lack of ego, and his recognition and appreciation of the worth of others.

It was certainly a unique, even a bizarre, project for a producer of wacky animated cartoons to undertake. In any event, the four-reel *Einstein's Theory of Relativity* was, surprisingly, an out-and-out success. The critics and the public applauded it. Max said that he understood that even Einstein was impressed and that he had written to the distributor that he thought the picture was an excellent attempt to illustrate an abstract subject. As he always did, Max took the acclaim modestly and liked to give a different version of what Einstein had said. He quotes

Einstein as saying: "Before this picture was made there were only seven people in the world who understood my theory of relativity. Now that Max Fleischer's movie has been made, nobody understands it!"

In 1925, the hottest topic of the time was the now-famous Scopes "monkey trial" taking place in Tennessee. A young schoolteacher named John Scopes was being tried there for teaching his pupils Darwin's theory of evolution. The trial was front-page news all over the country, especially since the prosecuting lawyer was William Jennings Bryan, one of the most prominent and flamboyant political personalities of the period. Leading the defense was the acknowledged finest lawyer in the profession, the legendary Clarence Darrow. The trial was a fight between science and religion, and since science was involved, Max was once again completely captivated. He decided to make another long film that would present the scientific argument for Darwin's theory. He contacted the American Museum of Natural History in New York and, with its cooperation and assistance, produced *Darwin's Theory of Evolution,* a five-reel feature combining animation and live action. Once again, the man who had earned his reputation making people laugh had taken on a profoundly serious subject.

The film was another surprise hit. Its first public screening was held in the Kaufman Theater of the American Museum of Natural History. My father and mother took me, at the tender age of nine, to that running of the picture, and I will never forget the experience. I remember nothing at all about the picture itself, but the huge, surging crowd of people trying to jam into the auditorium stays in my memory. There were hundreds of people outside trying to get in. The lobby of the theater was jam-packed with a rather unruly mob. Several museum display cases were knocked over and smashed. It came close to being a riot, and no one had yet seen the picture! The reception was pretty much the same wherever *Darwin's Theory of Evolution* played—large crowds filling the theaters, arguments and fistfights afterward. Max was a bit taken aback by the fuss his picture caused and became somewhat defensive. "In spite of the fact that the picture made an attempt to merely illustrate Darwin's theory and not to teach the theory," he wrote in his autobiography, "the picture was objected to by anti-Darwinites."

The fact that anyone was courageous enough to make films of both Einstein's theory and Darwin's theory, and was able to make them successfully, is remarkable enough. However, when you realize that those films were made by a man who had virtually no formal, conventional education, having attended only grammar school and art school, you can conclude only that that man was a genius.

As busy as the Out of the Inkwell studio was, a visit from Charles K. Harris, the well-known composer of "After the Ball," was about to make it even busier. In those silent movie days, the sing-along song slides were extremely popular. Every movie house had at least a pianist to supply music for the film being shown. The big theaters had not just an orchestra to accompany the picture, but even a mighty Wurlitzer organ. When slides with the lyrics of a popular song were projected on the screen, the audience would sing along with gusto, whether accompanied by a Wurlitzer or just a piano. Everyone just loved this part of the movie program. Everyone, that is, except Charles K. Harris. It bothered him that the musicians who accompanied the slides set the tempo, sometimes too fast, sometimes too slow, depending on their mood. Audiences would also frequently get out of synch with the lyrics when the projectionist was too early or too late with the next slide.

Harris happened to mention these annoying sing-along problems during his tour of the studio. Max saw the solution in an instant. Put the song lyrics, one line at a time, on motion picture film and project that film like an ordinary movie. But the crowning touch was his invention of the bouncing ball, a white ball that bounced from word to word. The phrase *follow the bouncing ball* has since become part of our language, and the image of the bouncing ball has imprinted itself on the world's memory. The bouncing ball is still in use in television advertising today. Not too long ago, during an interview with a press reporter, I mentioned that my father had invented the bouncing ball. The reporter's mouth dropped open. "Why," he exclaimed, "that's like saying he invented the hot dog!"

Max wasted no time in putting his invention into action. It was still in that busy year of 1924 when *Oh, Mabel,* the first in a long series of *Song Car-Tunes,* opened at the Circle Theatre in Manhattan. By this time, Max had embellished his bouncing ball concept so that, for variety, in place of the bouncing ball, the second chorus of the song had the delightful and very funny Ko-Ko the Clown leaping and dancing from word to word. And the words themselves got into the act. They changed shape, turning into animals; they melted, exploded, or suddenly vanished into thin air; but, whatever they did, it was always in perfect tempo.

Dick Huemer, one of the studio's very first animators, was present, along with Max and Dave, at the Circle Theatre opening. This is his report: "It brought down the house, it stopped the show. They applauded and stamped and whistled into the following picture, which they finally stopped and took off, and put back the 'Oh, Mabel' cartoon again. They ran it again to the delight of the audience. I always say that was an indication of what sound would do for animated cartoons."

The *Song Car-Tunes* became a hardy staple for the Out of the Inkwell studio.

6

There were three movie "palaces" in midtown Manhattan in the 1920s that hold a special place in my heart: the Rivoli, the Rialto, and the Criterion. They were what could be called a minicircuit since they were all under the supervision of Dr. Hugo Riesenfeld, a wild impresario and music conductor. Going to see a movie at any one of the three theaters was more than just an entertainment; it was an experience.

Each theater showed a different major motion picture, which was preceded by a huge theatrical production: dozens of elaborately costumed dancers; a full symphony orchestra; enormous sets. These productions were based on the theme of the picture and acted as a sort of mood-setting introduction to the feature that was to follow. These presentations were nothing less than spectacular. Incidentally, my sister, Ruth, who was at that time a beautiful, vivacious teenage dancer, was in the chorus at the Criterion.

I'm not sure how my father got connected with Riesenfeld, but I suspect it was through his old buddy from Bray Studios and the training-film stint at Fort Sill, Jack Leventhal. Somehow Leventhal had talked Riesenfeld into trying a real novelty with the Rialto Theatre orchestra, which Riesenfeld conducted. He proposed having an animated cartoon character conduct the live orchestra from the screen. Somewhere I've seen a still of a Fleischer cartoon character, baton in hand, in the act of conducting. If my memory serves me correctly, the Riesenfeld-Fleischer connection is clear. In any event, the unique, interactive happening was a sensation.

However it happened, one thing is clear. Riesenfeld was much taken with Max, so much so that he asked him to act as artistic and creative consultant for all the Rialto Theatre's productions. Max was far too busy to devote much time to this job, but he loved the theater and couldn't resist being a part of it. What it actually came down to was Max showing up for the final dress rehearsal, late at night, after the last showing of the current movie, and making suggestions about the new production. Since each show ran for about a month, it wasn't too demanding a job.

For me, the beauty part of the whole thing was that my father would always take my mother and me with him. About ten o'clock at night, we'd climb into our tiny, two-seater Studebaker in Brooklyn and, with me on my mother's lap, leap away from the curb. We were off to Manhattan and my beloved Rialto Theatre. I use *leap* accurately because that's the way that little car started. We nicknamed it "the Frog."

For a seven-year-old, the impact of what was happening onstage was overwhelming. It seemed like sheer chaos, and it was. Unfinished sets were being finished; lights were being hung and focused; color gels were being tested; the choreographer was pounding out the beat with a wooden staff and screaming out, "And one, and two, and three," while the chorus girls and boys were trying to dance and find their marks at the same time; the short, rotund figure of my father on the stage was pointing something out to the scenic designer. It seemed that everyone had something to shout about or run for. I watched it all wide-eyed, in a sea of empty theater seats, not understanding a thing, and loving every minute of it. I rarely got to see the curtain go up on the first run-through. By that time, my wide eyes were wide shut.

There was one final dress rehearsal that I'll never forget. It was 1925, and the Rialto was preparing the presentation for one of the last great silent movie classics, *The Vanishing American,* an American Indian epic starring Richard Dix. The theme of the presentation was, of course, the American Indian.

I was fast asleep in one of the theater seats when I was awakened by the loudest, most horrific crashing sound I've ever heard in my life. I think it sent me two feet into the air. It continued on and sounded as though the theater were collapsing. Suddenly, the curtains parted, and there, brilliantly spotlighted on the edge of the dark stage and coming head-on, directly at me, was a huge white horse running at full gallop and, riding on its back, an Indian warrior in war paint brandishing a tomahawk.

I sat there mouth agape, eyes very wide open, my hair standing straight up, for about ten seconds, and then the curtains closed, and the deafening sound eased off. There was applause, even cheers, from the cast and crew when the lights came back on and the curtain rose. I saw then what was causing the terrible noise. The horse was galloping on a wooden treadmill, and its hooves hitting the revolving, clattering, heavy wood slats made an unbelievably loud racket.

Everyone thought the effect was great except my father, who had just seen it for the first time. He got hold of the director, the stage manager, and the set designer. "You can't do that," he told them. "I absolutely will never give my approval for the staging of that scene. It has to be changed." They were incredulous. "But Max," they protested, "it's a smash opening for the presentation. You saw how effective it is. It's perfect! Why should we change it?" I could overhear the conversation, and even though I was very young, I thought they were right and my father was wrong. "I agree completely with everything you say," my father responded, "but you've overlooked one very simple thing." "What's that?" the director asked, with more than a hint of exasperation, which even I could detect. "Well," my father asked, "what would happen if, when the horse is going full gallop, the treadmill jammed?" The faces of the three men blanched perceptibly. My father continued: "That horse would come flying off that treadmill right into the orchestra pit and probably into the audience too."

The three were appalled. "Oh my God" was the only thing they could think of to say. Then, after a moment, the thoroughly shaken director asked: "What are we going to do?" "I've got a suggestion," my father said. "Instead of the horse coming head-on to the audience, why not have him profile? The action would be just as good, perhaps even better because you'd see all four legs in motion, and it'll be a heck of a lot safer." The three gents looked a bit dubious. "Okay," my father said, "why don't we take a look at it right now? All we have to do is turn the treadmill sideways, put the horse and rider on it, and say, 'Giddyap!'"

And that's what they did. They turned the treadmill sideways, put the horse and rider on it, and got the horse up to full gallop. The noise was just as frightening as before; the effect was terrific. Everything looked just great until the treadmill jammed. The horse and rider went flying off it as though shot out of a cannon, into the wings and into the stage wall. The horse was killed, and the rider, who jumped off at the last moment, went to the hospital with some broken bones. It was a smash opening, all right, but it never got to open. It was dropped from the presentation.

An interesting sidelight on the Riesenfeld connection is that Riesenfeld was also a friend of Dr. Lee DeForest, the eminent scientist who invented the radio vacuum tube. The tube made radio broadcasting possible as well as the amplification of sound. Lack of proper amplification had always been the greatest enemy of the development of sound films. DeForest was also one of the pioneers in the development of talking pictures and, in fact, was actually producing synchronized-sound short subjects called Phonofilms. Much to his credit, Riesenfeld introduced DeForest to Max. Both Max and DeForest saw the value of synchronized sound for Max's silent bouncing ball *Song Car-Tunes*. Together they made several sound-tracked *Song Car-Tunes,* starting with the 1924 *My Old Kentucky Home*. Strangely enough, the public didn't show much interest, and theater owners thought it a basically impractical idea since special equipment was required to show the films. Max was disappointed that the experiment in sound didn't work, but he could still release the films that he'd made as conventional silent shorts, and he also had the satisfaction of knowing that he'd made the first sound cartoon. Disney's *Steamboat Willie* usually gets the credit for being the first sound cartoon, but Max's *My Old Kentucky Home* preceded it by four years.

7

Taking a page from his former employer J. R. Bray's book, Max put the studio into high gear when, in 1923, he formed his own distribution company, Red Seal Pictures, with the plan to make all sorts of films other than cartoons. He hired Edwin Miles Fadiman, who was experienced in the distribution field, to run the company and committed to an ambitious release schedule of 120 short subjects.

Things started out well for Red Seal Pictures, and it looked like Max and Fadiman had a successful operation going. By 1925, Red Seal was releasing *Out of the Inkwell* cartoons, *Song Car-Tunes,* a new cartoon series called *Inkwell Imps* featuring Ko-Ko and his dog Fitz, and various live-action featurettes. One of the main productions was a live-action series called *Carrie of the Chorus,* a two-reel "backstage" showbiz comedy. My sister, Ruth, played the sidekick to the leading character, Carrie, and Ray Bolger played the male lead.

In 1924, Red Seal released twenty-six films. In 1925, it released 141 shorts. It wasn't too long, however, before Max and Fadiman realized that they were going to be hard put to continue to meet the production schedule to which they were committed. So Max took another page from J. R. Bray's book. Unfortunately, it was the wrong page: Red Seal began buying already-made films from small companies and releasing them under its own banner. These films didn't perform as hoped. It seems like the more Red Seal bought, the more it lost.

Problems started to crop up in the company: overhead expenses climbed to an unrealistic level; major disagreements arose with Fadiman, who finally quit. By 1926, Red Seal and Out of the Inkwell Films were broke. They couldn't pay their bills, and the film laboratory that processed their films refused to release their negatives until they were paid.

No one seems to know where Alfred Weiss came from, but in November 1926, shortly after Max asked for the appointment of a receiver in bankruptcy, Weiss crawled out of the woodwork and offered to take over Red Seal and Inkwell, pay their bills, and put them back in business. He seemed heaven-sent. He wasn't. He was, however, the only wheel in town, and Max felt that he had to go for it. Weiss became the president of both Red Seal and Inkwell. Max was hired on as vice president and Dave as art director, at salaries of two hundred dollars a week each with scheduled increases up to three hundred dollars per week.

On the basis of Max's name and reputation, Weiss wangled a distribution contract out of Paramount Pictures. The Red Seal company was abandoned. Weiss changed the name of Out of the Inkwell Films to "Inkwell Studios" and took the grand screen credit "PRESENTED BY" for himself. Finally, he changed the well-established *Out of the Inkwell* series name to *Inkwell Imps*. The studio started releasing *Inkwell Imps* and *Song Car-Tunes* through Paramount.

To cut a long and depressing story short, Max and Dave found it impossible to work for Weiss and quit the company. Shortly after they resigned, Weiss declared bankruptcy and disappeared.

Max and Dave were well and truly in deep trouble. They had barely enough money to hire one or two animators but not enough to rent studio space. Things were what can best be described as bleak—until, one night, my father came home looking somehow strange. I suppose I'd never before seen him with an expression of shock on his face. He came into the kitchen and said to my mother: "Essie, sit down. I've got something to tell you." She sat down, looking puzzled and a little scared. My father seemed to be fighting back some inner emotion. Then, quietly, he told her the news. A dear friend of his, Frank Goldman, one of the owners of Carpenter-Goldman, a film-processing laboratory based in Long Island City, had heard of the fix Max was in and had offered him space in his company's quarters for free—and for as long as he wanted it.

My mother sat there dumbfounded for a moment, then slowly put her hands to her mouth and started to cry. My father stood there, his lower lip trembling, his eyes blinking as they filled with tears. She got up and embraced him. He was now laughing and crying at the same time, and so was she. It was a tableau that has never faded from my mind. I was thirteen at the time and old enough to recognize that my father's reaction was not simply one of relief but one of being tremendously touched by the friendship of Frank Goldman.

In early April 1929, Max started a new studio in the Carpenter-Goldman space in Long Island City. It was called Fleischer Studios, the name the studio uses even today. The new company started making the only thing it could afford, *Song Car-Tunes*. Luckily, Max had kept the ownership of his creations Ko-Ko the Clown and the bouncing ball. Almost as important, he had also kept the relationship that Weiss had established with Paramount Pictures.

The advent of sound did wonders for the *Song Car-Tunes* and the bouncing ball. With his track record of successful and popular Ko-Ko the Clown cartoons and his unique knowledge of working with sound-on-film cartoons, Max was now able to exploit his relationship with Paramount Pictures. He concluded a new pact with the company to finance and distribute all Fleischer Studios productions.

Desperate times dictate desperate measures, and Max desperately needed Paramount to get him back in business. He was able to keep ownership of all the characters that he and the studio had created, but Paramount would actually own all the cartoons that he made for them. It was a deal much regretted later.

By the end of 1929, Fleischer Studios was back in its old spacious quarters at 1600 Broadway.

8

The addition of sound to the Fleischer cartoons also brought another addition to the roster of Fleischer brothers working at the studio. A highly talented, dedicated musician, my Uncle Lou was a perfect fit as head of the Music Department. Since the cartoons now contained wall-to-wall music, Lou became one of the busiest and most valuable men in the company.

Even though other producers' cartoons already had sound tracks, they didn't actually "talk." There was music, to be sure, but the cartoon characters made grunts, groans, or strangling sounds. Max decided to make cartoons that actually said words. This new series would be called *Talkartoons*. Paramount became so excited by the idea that it took out a trade-paper advertisement that read: "Paramount TALKARTOONS are something entirely new and entirely different from anything ever seen and heard before. For the first time cartoons will be actual talking pictures. . . ."

With the albatross of Red Seal Pictures off his back, the weight of Alfred Weiss off his feet, and the fresh air of the new Paramount deal in his lungs, Max began to reconceive Fleischer Studios. To differentiate the new regime from the old, he changed the name of the highly successful but newly sound-embellished *Song Car-Tunes* to *Screen Songs*. The musical bouncing ball cartoons became an astounding, wildly successful, runaway hit.

Ko-Ko, as happens to most older movie stars, was pushed off center stage by a new Walt Disney character called Mickey Mouse. Max's answer to this threat was to replace Ko-Ko's small mischievous dog, Fitz, with another canny canine. This was a much tougher, cigar-chewing, somewhat lecherous, piano-playing jazz hound named Bimbo (after my pet dog), meant to be Mickey's competition and complete opposite. Unfortunately, by the time the sixth *Talkartoon*, the 1930 *Dizzy Dishes*, went into production, it was clear that even Bimbo's big feet weren't filling Mickey's shoes. There was something missing—a love interest. And that was when Max came up with his greatest creation of all, Betty Boop.

The script for *Dizzy Dishes* called for a female entertainer to play opposite Bimbo. Since Bimbo was a dog, Max devised a character that was half dog and half human female. In its first appearance, the character was nameless, but what a character it was—gross, ugly, with an enormous, bouncy behind. However, it did have round, saucer-like eyes and shapely feminine legs.

The executives at Paramount flipped for the dog-lady and wanted more films made with her. Max was delighted to oblige and made her the lead in every cartoon. But Max immediately began to work with his animators on refining the character. The dog-like features didn't last very long. The flabby mouth began to look human, the dog snout became a little dot of a nose, and the gross figure became very sexy, with a tiny waist and a very human bosom. By her ninth picture, *Minding the Baby*, the character had lost her dog ears, acquiring in their place hoop earrings, and come to look completely human. *Minding the Baby* also marks the first time the character was given a name—Betty Boop—and, with that picture, the *Talkartoon* series was renamed the *Betty Boop* series.

Once more, Max Fleischer had a genuine, honest-to-God hit on his hands. Betty epitomized the Jazz Age. Max had the top jazz artists of the time appear in her cartoons, figures such as Cab Calloway and Louis Armstrong. A host of other great entertainers also joined the fun, among them Ethel Merman and Rudy Vallee. Without question, Max's *Screen Songs* and *Talkartoon/Betty Boop* series were the forefathers of the then distant MTV.

Merchandising took off with Betty Boop dolls, clothes, dishes, fan clubs, you name it. The character had her own daily comic strip and a Sunday strip as well. The Bamberger Broadcasting System carried a weekly fifteen-minute coast-to-coast Betty Boop radio show called *Betty Boop Fables*. The whole world, it seemed, had fallen in love with Betty Boop.

Several squeaky female voices were tried out in the early *Betty Boops,* but none seemed exactly right. The voice needed to be squeaky, but it also needed to be cute and sexy, to sing, to do good line readings, and to be able to say and sing "Boop-oop-a-doop" in exactly the right way. Max finally found what he was looking for in 1931 when he came across the incomparable Mae Questel. Her voice and Betty Boop became synonymous. Oddly enough, Mae looked exactly like Betty Boop. She stayed with the series until its end, 118 pictures later.

Since my father's death in 1972, Grim Natwick, one of Fleischer Studios' oldest and most talented animators, has often been quoted as claiming to be the creator of Betty Boop. But, before his death, my father had sworn under oath in two lawsuits that he, Max Fleischer, was the sole creator of the character. He acknowledged that many animators contributed to her development, not just Natwick, but also Seymour Kneitel, Myron Waldman, Doc Crandall, Ted Sears, Willard Bowsky, and Al Eugster. I find it more than passing strange that, to my knowledge at least, Natwick never made such a claim while my father was alive.

9

Clearly, Max was riding the crest of a wave. Who would have thought that the sassy, ugly mutt from *Dizzy Dishes* would metamorphose into America's sweetheart, and Europe's, and the rest of the world's too? But it turned out that an even bigger wave was right behind him.

Max couldn't help but notice the great popularity of the leading character, Popeye the Sailor, in Elzie Segar's *Thimble Theatre* daily comic strip. He had a strong hunch that the one-eyed, funny-looking sailor might work just as well, or even better, on the silver screen as he did in the confines of a comic strip. On November 17, 1932, Max signed a contract with King Features Syndicate, the owner of the rights to the character. King Features was not at all sure that this whole concept would work and demanded that a "test cartoon" be made and shown in theaters before May 30, 1933.

Depending on the positive reception of the test, the contract called for a payment to King of $500 for the first cartoon in a twelve-picture series and 17.5 percent of the gross in excess of $31,500. Merchandising rights were not included in the deal. What was included, however, was a paragraph that absolutely floored me when I read it while researching this chapter. Shorn of its legal lingo, that paragraph says, quite simply, that after ten years of exhibition the "Producer" will furnish to the "Owner" (King Features) proof by affidavit that "all negatives and duplicate negatives and all positive prints, copies, reproductions and duplicates thereof, shall be destroyed."

The first thing that comes to mind is, What could they have been thinking of? This is sheer lunacy! They certainly weren't thinking of television. But then who was? When you put yourself in the mind-set of the pretelevision 1930s, what else would you do with a bunch of old cartoons that had played themselves out in first, second, and even third runs other than junk them? Who could have foreseen the mind-boggling concept of movies flying through the air right onto a screen in your living room and then being shown over and over again? Who knew?

As it stood, considering the naïveté of the time, that clause in the contract seemed innocent enough. Eventually, it turned out to be a time bomb of devastating, catastrophic proportions.

A lot was riding on the test cartoon. Max, Dave, and the top animators had to make life-and-death decisions in order to successfully transfer the static comic strip *Popeye* to the dynamics of the movie screen. What kind of walk should Popeye have? What kind of voice? Should he have a theme song? Where does his strength come from? Interestingly enough, in the comic strip, Popeye's strength came from rubbing the head of a magic whiffle hen, not from eating spinach. The superstrength-giving spinach, which became Popeye's trademark, was strictly a Fleischer Studios' contribution. Switching from the whiffle hen to spinach was probably the most important creative decision that Max had to make in constructing the character of the movie Popeye. But there were dozens of others to be made as well, and any misjudgment could mean the failure of the project.

It was decided not to launch Popeye on his own but to give him a sort of screen test by introducing him in a *Betty Boop* cartoon titled *Popeye the Sailor*. I was in the Paramount Theatre in Manhattan on July 14, 1933, when Popeye made his first appearance on the screen. It was another memorable opening. Every bit of comic action, from Popeye's peculiar galloping gait to his topping off the first line of his signature song, "I'm Popeye the Sailor Man," with a mighty "TOOT" from his pipe, was greeted with uproarious laughter and sheer delight from the audience.

What surprised me then, at seventeen, and still surprises me today was that the Fleischer gang didn't play this picture safe. They took chances that only loony animators would take. Near the opening of the picture, Popeye does a sort of hornpipe arm gesture of hiking up his trousers that reveals that he is wearing a tightly laced, old-fashioned corset that pinches in his waist and puffs out his chest, making him look more manly. A little later on, he does a very unmanly, but very sexy, Hawaiian hula dance with a clearly topless Betty Boop. There may be chancier ways to introduce a well-loved, well-established character in his movie debut, but I can't think of any.

The *Popeye* series took off like a scalded cat. Up to that point, Betty Boop had been Mickey Mouse's only competitor. Eventually, Popeye became more popular than even the mouse.

It was nothing but blue skies for Max, Dave, and Fleischer Studios—except for one small cloud.

Mae Questel, Betty's voice, was not the only one who looked like Betty Boop. The popular singer Helen Kane looked like her too. But then so did the movie star Clara Bow, the "It" girl. And so did many thousands of other women. It wasn't surprising since that particular look—the "boyish" bob, the spit curls, the round face, the wide, mascaraed eyes—was very popular in the late 1920s and the 1930s.

According to Helen Kane, the problem was not that she looked like Betty Boop but that Betty Boop looked like her, sang like her, and, most important, used the phrase *Boop-oop-a-doop,* which Kane claimed to have invented. In April 1934, Kane sued Max Fleischer, Fleischer Studios, and Paramount Pictures for $250,000, on the grounds that her *Boop-oop-a-doop* had been wrongfully appropriated from her, with a resulting loss in income. Ironically, in one of the *Betty Boop* cartoons, Betty pleads euphemistically for the villain to spare her virginity by singing: "You can feed me bread and water / Or a great big bale of hay / But don't take my Boop-oop-a-doop away." Although Kane's accusations strangely mirrored the cartoon, my father, Fleischer Studios, and Paramount remained undaunted by her claims that they had taken her *Boop-oop-a-doop* away.

The trial itself, although deadly serious for the principals involved, seems to have been a sort of comic opera. The newspapers had a ball with it. Even the staid *New York Times* carried a headline that read: "COURT SOLEMN AS HELEN KANE BOOPS OUT GRIEF."

At one point in the trial, the *Times* reported, Kane's lawyer directed her to remove her hat and coat "so the court might see if her face and figure resembled that of Betty of the cartoon. To make the resemblance more striking she arranged locks of her hair across her temples and cheeks. Young women in the audience immediately began practicing the coiffure." That same article also reports: "Several photographs of Miss Kane on song sheets that also contained ecstatic descriptions of her, were introduced. Justice McGoldrick remarked: 'Of course, I shall consider only the pictures, but I suppose counsel will have no objection if I try the music on the piano.' He said he would have no difficulty in considering the pictures alone, because they were obviously the prettiest parts of the sheets. 'Thank you,' piped Miss Kane."

I've also been told by my father, who was an avid spectator in the courtroom, that some days of the trial were actually hilarious, especially those when the lawyers, all well past middle age, started arguing about whether the phrase in question was *Boop-oop-a-doop, Boop-boop-de-boop, Boop-a-doop-oop, Boopy-doop-a-doop,* or whatever.

Eventually, a piece of sound film made in 1928 was dredged up proving that a black nightclub entertainer named Baby Esther was singing *Boop-oop-a-doop* long before Helen Kane. The judge ruled that Kane had failed to prove that the defendants wrongfully appropriated her technique and ruled against her.

10

The fortunes of the Fleischer family seemed to run counter to the times. Wall Street laid an egg in 1929, and the Great Depression overtook the country and the world—but not Max. The Depression was the period of his greatest successes, and instead of going broke like everyone else, Max was starting to make money. That was because, during the Depression, the worried populace sought escape from their problems in the entertainment that was to be found in movie houses.

The first noticeable improvement in our family's way of life was the move from our modest apartment at 1678 Union Street in Brooklyn to a much classier address, 589 Eastern Parkway. No more ordinary apartment house now. We had moved to a brownstone on a wide boulevard with a landscaped median strip running down the center, not unlike Park Avenue in Manhattan.

Apparently, we weren't quite well enough off to have the brownstone all to ourselves. It was a three-story building, and we occupied the bottom two floors. Two maiden-lady seam-stresses resided quietly on the third. The only excitement they ever caused was one night when they came racing hysterically down into our place to tell us that there was a prowler in their flat. My father called the cops while we all waited breathlessly outside. Eventually, a single policeman showed up and entered the darkened house to investigate. About a minute later, we heard two shots fired, and about a minute after that, the cop came bursting out of the house, gun in hand, and in an absolute fury. "Who," he screamed at us, "was stupid enough to leave a dressmaker's dummy at the top of the stairs?"

Betty Boop kept booping, and Max felt secure enough to make another upward jump in our lifestyle. We moved to an apartment building called the Theodore Roosevelt at 125 Eastern Parkway, the swankiest part of the street. It really was a great location, directly across the parkway from the Brooklyn Museum of Art and the Brooklyn Botanical Gardens. I spent a lot of my youth in both those places.

Another sign of our growing affluence was that my father sold the Frog, the little Studebaker that leaped away from the curb, and got a much bigger and grander car. Typical of him, it wasn't an ordinary car. An extraordinary man needs an extraordinary car. Max bought a Jackson. I believe that only twelve of these cars were ever made. A Jackson closely resembled, and was frequently mistaken for, a convertible Rolls Royce. When the top was up and you ignored the isinglass windows, it looked like a tank since the chassis was heavily studded with rivets. But it was a powerful vehicle with a powerful company motto: "No hill too steep, no mud too deep!" Our car at least lived up to that motto, and when it was sold, it was bought by an auto repair shop and converted into a tow-car. Eventually it became a hearse.

The continuing success of Betty Boop, plus the additional booster rocket of Popeye, finally pushed us into the financial stratosphere. My father bought a twelve-cylinder Packard limousine and hired a chauffeur to drive it. This was all pretty heady stuff, but it wasn't yet the apogee. My father decided to move us to Manhattan.

I was with my mother and father on one of their apartment-hunting forays into New York. I was then about fifteen and remember it well because my father made one of the all-time great puns. We were looking at apartments in the Windermere Hotel, an apartment-hotel at West End Avenue and Ninety-second Street. We were in one that overlooked the Hudson River when my father asked the rental agent how much the river-view apartments cost. The agent explained that the prices varied depending on how good a view you had of the river. The higher up you went, the better the view, the more it cost. My father went over to the window, gazed out of it for a moment, and then said: "River, stay 'way from my dough."

So we moved into apartment 11J at the Windermere. It had a nice view of the river.

11

Several times during the writing of these pages I have quoted from my father's unpublished autobiography. A reader may wonder why I'm going to all the trouble of writing a biography of Max Fleischer when an autobiography already exists. Well, the autobiography, written in 1939, is all of nine pages long. It is so crammed with condensed facts and philosophies that reading it is akin to trying to make a meal out of a bouillon cube.

For example, Max describes his working habits in just these few lines: "Working hours are from 8 A.M. to 12 and 1 to 5. But I never stop. I never did need more than four hours sleep. I usually get that from two to six A.M. As a rule sleep very soundly." About recreation he writes: "Outside of work and bowling, the thing I'm most fond of is the theatre. I play the mandolin— when no one is around. The missus says I play it for my own 'amazement.' I can't play one complete song. While I'm playing I do forget about business."

So far the portrait that I've tried to paint of my father has concentrated on his inventive and creative mind, but that portrait is incomplete and will probably remain so. I can't supply all the lines necessary for the whole to emerge, only some of the colors. Still, when the colors come together, like the dots of a pointillist painting, perhaps something resembling Max Fleischer will emerge.

My parents lived in apartment 11J in the Windermere for many years and never gave a thought to living anywhere else. Why should they? Here they had a fine apartment with full hotel service: maids; laundry; room service; a valet. The only irritant for my father was Sam, the valet. Sam was sloppy. The laundry would be delivered with shirts missing buttons and trousers poorly pressed. I was there one day when Sam made a delivery and my father found a shirt collar badly done. Max was not a man given to sudden bursts of temper, but this time he let poor Sam have it. He gave him a stern lecture about taking pride in his work and ended up by asking: "Don't you want to be known as the best tailor in New York?" To which Sam answered: "No."

My father was truly shocked. Then he started to laugh. I had never seen him laugh so heartily. Finally, he put his arm around the bewildered Sam's shoulders and ushered him to the door, saying: "Okay, Sam. Forget it." I heard my father tell this story over and over again. He always laughed at the punch line. It seems that it had never occurred to him that anyone could be perfectly happy not being the best there was at whatever he was doing. He wasn't laughing at Sam; he was laughing at himself.

A lot of things happened over the years in 11J, but none more bizarre than what happened during one long, hot summer. I call it the nature in the raw episode. My sister, Ruth, was by this time married to Seymour Kneitel, one of Fleischer Studios' top animators. Ruth and Seymour had their own apartment, not too far away from the Windermere. It was the hottest part of a very hot summer, and they were planning a vacation in the mountains. Their pride and joy was a brilliantly colored lovebird that they had bought in Havana on their honeymoon. There was a great deal of sentiment attached to this little bird.

Not wanting to take the bird with them, Ruth and Seymour brought it over to the folks' place for safekeeping. My mother and father promised to take care of it as though it were the crown prince of Romania. Residential air-conditioning was not yet common, and the apartment, like every other apartment in New York, was stiflingly hot. After Ruth and Seymour left on their trip, my father felt that the bird looked a little wilted from the heat. He placed its cage in the only spot where it could get what little breeze there was—on the sill of one of the open bedroom windows facing the river. He even pulled up the metal venetian blind so that the bird got not only the breeze but a lovely view of the New Jersey shoreline on the other side of the Hudson as well.

My father went into the dining room for a bit of lunch, then decided to check on the bird's water supply. As he stepped into the bedroom, he was greeted by a very strange sight. The birdcage on the windowsill was entirely covered with what appeared to be a shiny black cloth. My father was completely puzzled. He slowly approached the black-shrouded cage, trying to figure out what was on it and how it got there. When he got close enough, he reached out a tentative hand and touched it. The black cloth gave a dreadful screech and exploded into a horrifying vision of huge flapping wings, big, beady eyes, grasping claws, and a vicious beak—and flew away.

My father gave a startled yell and then realized what had happened. It was a marauding hawk from the bonnie banks of the Jersey swampland across the river. The flashy colors of the little bird had advertised it as a tasty morsel, and the hawk went for it, wrapping its black wings around the birdcage for support. But then the real horror of the situation presented itself. There, lying on the bottom of the cage, was the beloved lovebird, decapitated.

It was at this moment that my mother ran into the room to see what the commotion was about. She took one look and passed out. So much for the safekeeping of the crown prince of Romania.

My father got angry. Really angry. Angry enough to use curse words, which was a great rarity for him. He vowed he'd get that son of a bitch of a hawk. "He knows that our bird is still there in the cage," he reasoned. "If we give him another chance at it, he'll come back. That's when I'll get him. He'll never fly again, believe me."

Early the next morning he set the bait. He glued the head back on the bird's body and wired the legs onto its little swing perch. Getting it to stand upright instead of hanging upside down took some engineering, but he was good at that. Then he placed the cage back in the same place on the windowsill it had been when it was attacked.

His plan was to stand with his back flattened against the wall alongside the window where he couldn't be seen from the outside, with his fist raised high above his head. When the hawk came back to get the bird, he'd bring his fist down with a mighty blow and smash that son of a bitch of a hawk.

My mother pleaded with him not to go on with his mad plan: the hawk might never come back; it might attack him instead of the lovebird; if he missed, he might fall out the window. My father would have none of it. He was going to do battle with the beast, and that was that. My mother threw her hands up in disgust. "He's crazy," she said, marching out of the room.

My father took off his shirt and stood in his undershirt, his body glistening slightly from the heat and the excitement. Although he was strong, he didn't exactly have a caveman's body. He was only five foot five tall and had a pretty large tummy, which was called a corporation at that time. He wrapped a towel around his right fist, then took up his position against the wall alongside the window, his wrapped fist held high, and waited.

It was a ridiculous situation. The law of the jungle had taken over. This was nature in the raw, man against beast, a fight to the death in the concrete canyons of Manhattan.

The tableau was motionless. Then the incredible happened. In less than a minute a shadow passed over the window. A few seconds later it passed again, and then again. And suddenly there it was, the hawk, its claws reaching forward, its wings closing around the cage. My father muttered through clenched jaws, "You son of a bitch!" raised his toweled fist a bit higher for more force, and aimed a mighty blow at the monstrous bird. And then it happened. The towel wrapped around his fist got caught in the metal venetian blind, and the whole damn thing came crashing down on my father, knocking him to the floor, and entangling him in the slats. The hawk flew back to New Jersey now knowing how dangerous it was to go hunting in New York.

My father bought a new lovebird and tried painting it to make it look like the old one, but it didn't work. When they came to retrieve the bird, Ruth and Seymour spotted the phony right away. They were not amused by the story.

My father was a man of routines and habits, some of them rather strange. One of them was that he loved dirty drugstores. No kidding. In those days almost all drugstores had a soda fountain. Wherever we moved, including the two moves we made when we lived in Miami Beach, Max would find out where the nearest dirty drugstore was, and that's where we'd go just about every night.

The floors in these places that Max loved were unkempt, littered with crumpled paper napkins, gum wrappers, squashed cigarette butts, and other drugstore rubbish. We nicknamed them "the DDs." And then there was the smell: a musty mixture of medicinal preparations and the sweet odors of various syrups from the soda fountain. In the evening, all my father would have to do was raise his eyebrows and say "DD?" and off we'd go. Why he loved these places we never could figure out, but he insisted on going to the DD every night for his chocolate-ice-cream sundae with chocolate sauce. And we all went with him.

One of my father's best-loved routines was daily lunch with some of the animators. They'd walk to Roth's Grill on Seventh Avenue, directly behind the studio at 1600 Broadway. True to his compulsive nature, Max ordered the same thing every day, a hot open-faced thick roast beef sandwich, with plenty of gravy and mashed potatoes. The fact that he would always splatter himself with gravy was a great source of amusement to the animators, who liked to give him some good-natured ribbing. My mother was not as forgiving as the animators and would give him hell about his sloppiness.

Finally, one day, he decided to reform. At the start of lunch, he told the group that he was tired of getting bawled out at home and kidded so much by his friends. "So," he said, "I want you to observe me carefully today, and you will see a new Max. No more spots on my tie or anyplace else. You will see a demonstration of careful and elegant eating. Now, watch carefully." He picked up his knife and fork in a theatrically exaggerated manner, pinkies aloft, a high-society look on his face, and delicately cut off a tiny piece of the gravy-soaked beef. With a grand sweep of his arm he brought the morsel to his mouth. What he hadn't noticed was that the piece of beef on his fork was still attached to the main slab of meat by a thin ligament, and as the fork neared his mouth, the whole piece of meat rose off its plate like a flying carpet and landed flat on his chest, covering necktie, shirt, and coat lapels with gravy-laden, succulent beef.

So much for the new Max.

It's been a little uncomfortable for me in these pages to refer to my father as Max, even though he was called Max by everyone else in the world. In fact, he insisted on, and took pride in, being called Max by every one of his studio's employees, including the guy who mopped the floors and emptied the trash. Still, to my sister and me, it was unthinkable to call him anything other than Pops. Not Dad. Not Pop. But Pops. Pops it was, and Pops it would always be, even with him long gone and Ruth and I very senior citizens. Whenever we talked about him, he was still Pops.

Actually, I have to qualify my statement that I never called him anything other than Pops. We had a personal and secret language. When I was about six or seven, he started calling me Smiss or Smiss Boy, and I would always respond by calling him Smiss Pops. There was a popular song at that time called "I

Miss My Swiss (My Swiss Miss Misses Me)." Somehow I relate that song to our using those names. The song was meant as a tongue twister, and perhaps it was my mispronouncing the words that got things started. In any event, I clearly understood that *Smiss* was our code word for *smart*. When my father wrote to me when I was away at camp or on a trip with my mother and sister, he would always start the letter with "Dear Smiss." As far as he was concerned, that was my name.

The love between us was so great that we could never say good-bye to each other. We had to have special words for that. I haven't a clue as to how our routine got started, but on parting my father would say, "Solongus," and I would answer, "Pepsibongus." It just occurs to me now, as I'm writing this, that my father might have been saying, "So long, us," and I was just answering in rhyme.

My father was an early riser and left for the studio before I awoke to go to school. He never failed to open the door to my room and in a stage whisper say "Smiss Boy," and somehow I always heard it and responded with a mumbled "Smiss Pops." Then came the ritual "Solongus . . . Pepsibongus," after which he quietly closed the door.

Saying good-bye when we were both present wasn't too tough to do. Saying good-bye over the phone was something else. It was very funny and very difficult at the same time. It was a process that sometimes took several minutes because neither of us had the heart to hang up on the other. The process went something like this:

Pops: Well, solongus.
Me: Pepsibongus.

[*A long pause while we wait to hear the disconnect.*]

Pops: Go ahead, hang up.

Me: No, you hang up first.

Pops: Okay. I'm hanging up now.

Me: Okay.

Pops: Click!

[*We'd both laugh.*]

Pops: Now go ahead and hang up. No foolin'.

Me: Okay. [*Short pause.*] Click!

[*More laughter.*]

Pops: Okay. We'll both hang up on the count of three.

Me: Okay.

Pops: One! Two! Three!

Both of us: Click!

[*Laughter from both of us and, with a few variations, we'd start the process over until one of us finally gave up.*]

As Max mentions in his short autobiography, one of his favorite pastimes was playing the mandolin. Actually, he enjoyed playing all stringed instruments, like the banjo and even the Hawaiian guitar. The Fleischer family had a musical bent, and my grandfather, who was a pretty good violinist, taught all his children to play an instrument. My sister, Ruth, who was quite a bit older than I was, recalled that, when she was a child, every night my father's brothers and his sister, Ethel, would gather at our house and there would be a concert, with Ethel on the piano. They'd play classical music and cakewalks.

This musical tradition continued even after the studio moved to Florida. Not every night, of course, but at least one evening a week there'd be a musical gathering. After a while the ensemble playing began to taper off, but my father wouldn't give it up. He had the group record its repertoire on some phonograph records but without his part. After that he was able to play his instrument, usually the Hawaiian guitar, by himself but with the proper musical accompaniment on the Victrola. I would announce his concerts as "Max Fleischer and His Mechanical Friends!"

His other pastime was the theater. The theater to Max was the regular, so-called legitimate theater. Movies were not a pastime; they were a part of our daily lives. Going to the movies several times a week was routine. After dinner was the time to go. It didn't matter what was playing or when it started. We went. Arriving in the middle of a picture didn't matter. We'd sit through the two features—it was the time of the double feature and selected short subjects—a newsreel, a cartoon, a travelogue, and anything else that was showing, until a recognizable scene turned up. "This is where we came in," we'd tell each other, leave, and go to the DD.

The first movie I remember was a film that my father particularly wanted me to see. I was probably about seven, and he told me that it was something I had to see. He took me alone, during the day, to an "art-house theater." I never forgot the experience. The film was *The Cabinet of Doctor Caligari*. I still carry an image from it around in my head—a tall, pale-faced, thin man in a long black coat, his eyes circled in black, standing in a narrow hallway, its walls askew. I remember not so much being frightened as somehow being hypnotized by the image.

I've never really figured out why my father wanted me to see that surrealistic masterpiece. By no stretch of the imagination was it a film for children. Perhaps, with this film, he was initiating me into the world in which he lived. His animated cartoons always relied heavily on surrealism for their effect. Perhaps it was his way of stretching my imagination, of making me aware that there was more than one way of looking at reality.

The theater, however, was quite a different matter. We got dressed up in our best clothes, and there was a special feeling of excitement in the air. My father truly loved the theater. He must have been one of the first subscribers to the Theatre Guild, and I don't believe we missed a single one of the company's plays.

One of the productions that I remember vividly—it may have been the first play I ever saw—was Karel Capec's *R.U.R.* (i.e., Rossum's Universal Robots). That one scared the hell out of me and stuck in my emotional memory for the rest of my life. Another was the Marx brothers' *Coconuts*. I literally fell out of my seat laughing. The point is that my father believed in and loved the theater so much that he wanted me to experience everything it had to offer whether I understood it or not. He must have figured that some of it would stick with me. He may have been right.

Some priceless words of wisdom that my father gave me, when I was literally at his knee, were: "Never take a percentage of the profit. Take the money up front." Also: "The only way you'll see a profit from a movie is if they make so much money so fast they don't have time to hide it all."

Almost from the very beginning Walt Disney was an annoying pebble in my father's shoe, a pebble that eventually grew into a rock. Max never talked about it much, but Disney's constant winning of awards, for the beauty and graceful animation of his cartoons, rankled. It was well known in the industry that, because of the award-winning quality of Disney's cartoons, they were too expensive, and the Disney Company was frequently close to going broke. I once asked my father if he ever envied Disney's ability to cop so many accolades. His answer was straightforward and telling. "Just remember one thing," he said. "You can't eat medals."

In 1939, I had just completed my premed course at Brown University and was in a quandary. I didn't know whether to become a doctor or go into the theater. During my four years of premed, I had majored in psychology with the goal of becoming a psychiatrist. I was, in fact—and I say this with all due modesty—the best psychology student in the university. At the same time, however, I had pretty well immersed myself in the theater by writing sketches and directing and acting for the Brownbrokers, the university's musical comedy organization, and I'd loved every minute of it. I'd brought this love of theater with me from my prep school, where I was the head of the Drama Club.

So I was torn: med school or drama school? I had never before felt that I needed my father's advice in making a decision, but this time the stakes were pretty high. So I brought my problem to him. He was not surprised when I told him of my dilemma. He had seen it coming.

"What I think you should do," he told me, "is to find the toughest drama school you can find and go to it for a year. At the end of a year you'll either love the theater or you'll hate it. If you hate it, there's no harm done; you're still qualified to go to medical school. All you've lost is a year. But look what happens if you don't go and try it out. You'll be unhappy for the rest of your life, not knowing if the theater was your true calling. You'll always have a lingering doubt about whether medicine was really the right profession for you, and that's no way to live."

The Bible says that the price of wisdom is above rubies. I went to the Yale School of Drama and lived happily ever after.

12

Although this book is primarily about Max Fleischer, there was an Essie Fleischer too. When Max and Essie took their marriage vows in 1905, they really meant it—especially the "until death do us part" promise. Death parted them sixty-five years later.

Essie was a five foot three firecracker with a constantly smoking short fuse and a slightly broken nose that was never properly set. She got that when she passed out in the bathroom of our Union Street apartment while she was pregnant with me. It was not just her fuse that kept smoking but she herself, a chain-smoker, just like Max. What makes it noteworthy is that she started smoking before it became popular for women to do so in public. Years later, when women experimented with cigars and pipes, Essie was out there puffing away with the best of them.

But that was typical of Essie, always avant-garde. There is a daring photograph of her on a summer holiday in the Catskill

Mountains, in the early 1920s, wearing voluminous skirts that she has pulled back between her legs so that it looks like she's wearing men's trousers.

Bridge and mah-jongg were games that ladies played. My mother organized a poker club with her women friends. She loved gambling, any kind. She got interested in horse racing and made occasional trips out to the Narragansett racetrack, not all that far from Manhattan. Even after she found a bookie, she still went to the track. She loved watching the horses run and the excitement of rooting home the very occasional winner. She got a special kick out of the races because a relative of ours was Bobby Merit, a well-known, top professional jockey. He'd phone her with tips every once in a while. Mostly they didn't work, but she was thrilled with feeling that she was on the inside.

When Fleischer Studios eventually moved to Miami, Florida, my mother was not at all unhappy. She loved Miami Beach, and Hialeah racetrack was close by. Our family moved into an impressively large two-story house in Miami Beach. One of the first things my mother did was to get herself a bookie.

On the days she couldn't get to Hialeah, she'd keep that bookie busy. Her big problem was that she loved to be out on our rather extensive grounds among the exotic plants and not close to a phone to place bets and get results. Her solution was quite simple. She had phones installed on the trunks of several of the many palm trees. The effect on uninitiated visitors was quite startling, particularly if they were in the pergola. From their point of view, it looked like my mother was talking to a tree.

My mother had a very good operatic singing voice. It was untrained, but she could really sing. Whenever there was a large, formal family event, usually a wedding or a bar mitzvah, there would be, without fail, a call for Essie to sing after dinner was finished. It didn't take much urging. Up she'd get and, without any accompaniment, belt out the same song every time, "Ah, Sweet Mystery of Life (at Last I've Found Thee)." I sat in dread of the last line, "For it is love alone that lives for aye!" which ended on a high C. It is an impossibly high note. I always feared she wouldn't make it, that she'd be off-key, or that her voice would crack, that there would be a great embarrassment, a humiliation. But the only things that cracked were any nearby glasses. She hit the high C every time. It would get her a standing ovation, and she never failed to amaze me.

Someone once asked Dame Sybil Thorndike if she'd ever thought of divorcing her husband: Her response: "Divorce? No! Murder? Yes!" That pretty much applies to my parents' relationship. Theirs was a long marriage but not a particularly smooth one. In fact, it sometimes got pretty rocky. There were some good shouting matches, with my mother doing by far most of the shouting. I seem to remember a dent in a kitchen wall that was made by a coffee pot that she winged at my father.

These contretemps were usually brought on by Essie's violent fits of jealously. She was very much in love with Max, and there were fairly frequent accusations of his "making eyes" at some young lady. I remember one such incident when she accused him of making a pass at the wife of the local DD's owner. For once, he did more shouting than she did.

My father, I believe, shrugged off the accusations and the blowups. But Essie took them all very seriously—so much so that one day, when I was about six or seven and we were still living on Union Street, she attempted suicide. She went into the bathroom one morning and tried to swallow a bottle of iodine. It was a very poor choice of lethal weapon. As soon as the liquid hit the inside of her mouth, it burned like hell. She spat it out and started screaming in panic. My sister, Ruth, a teenager at that point, rushed into the bathroom and also started screaming. My mother was flailing around, with Ruth trying to find out what had happened and keep Essie from hurting herself. Neighbors started rushing into the room yelling: "What happened? What happened?"

I guess that's why I remember the incident even though I was so young. For me, the screaming and the bedlam were traumatic. Ruth, or a neighbor, called an ambulance. By the time it arrived, Essie had rinsed her mouth and calmed down and was insisting that it was just an accident, that she had mistakenly picked up the wrong bottle of medicine. But who takes medicine right out of the bottle?

Essie never tried anything like that again. There were no more superdramatic gestures. This suicide incident was very much out of character for her. I never remember her being depressed. Angry and volatile, yes. Morbid and gloomy, no. In fact, she was the life of every party. She got things moving with her singing and dancing. She did a mean Charleston. Her drink of choice was Scotch, neat—no water, no soda, no ice, just Scotch.

Travel was another big favorite of hers. From 1929 on she took Ruth and me to Europe every summer. That's where she started to smoke small cigars. But there was nothing she liked more than a good dirty story—the dirtier, the better. And she had a laugh that was both irrepressible and contagious. Once it got going, there was no stopping it. You'd think she was finished laughing, but usually she wasn't. A few seconds later, the laugh would start to bubble out of her, and she'd try to suppress it. There is nothing more contagious than a suppressed laugh. It makes everyone else start to snicker and, if it goes on long enough, laugh out loud.

This frequently had a devastating effect during a movie or a play. Along with the rest of the audience, she'd start to laugh at something. Then, after everyone else had stopped, they'd hear a suppressed giggle, then another, and another. Soon someone else would start to giggle, then someone else; then the entire audience would break into laughter. It didn't matter if the film or the play was now involved in a serious moment; the audience would be howling with laughter. At those moments, I would gladly have strangled my mother.

My mother outlived my father by many years. On her hundredth birthday, we had a party for her at the Motion Picture Country House in Woodland Hills, California, where she was living. What with her children and her children's children, it made quite a gathering. She was in fine fettle: clear minded, sharp, alert.

After the birthday cake was finished, I said to her: "Mom, I've got a little, special present for you. Something you haven't had for a long, long time." I reached into my pocket and brought out a small bottle filled with an amber fluid. "How would you like a little nip of Scotch?"

Her eyes brightened, and her face lit up in a broad smile. "You bet!" she exclaimed. I unscrewed the top and handed her the little bottle. She took it from me, held it high, and made a toast. Then she took a nice sip of Scotch as she always did, neat.

We all watched her swallow, waiting for her reaction. It came. Her eyes widened; she dropped the bottle; she grasped her throat and started to strangle. She was fighting for breath. At first, it was horrible gasping and gagging; then she went into a fit of loud, uncontrollable coughing. We stood there horrified, helpless. Somebody screamed out: "Get a nurse!" But nurses were already running toward us. She finally coughed herself out, her eyes streaming tears, and got her breath back. We were all shaken, especially me. All I could think of was a newspaper headline that would read: "HOLLYWOOD MOVIE DIRECTOR KILLS MOTHER ON 100TH BIRTHDAY."

Essie made it to 103. On her passing, I toasted her with a small shot of Scotch. Neat.

One of Max's early editorial cartoons (1902) for the *Brooklyn Daily Eagle*.

Max Fleischer (left) posed next to his older brother Charlie, late 1880s.

Left: Not one of William Fleischer's stuffed horses, but close. (Max Fleischer illustration, 1900.) *Right: Brooklyn Daily Eagle* cartoon, 1902, by Max Fleischer.

Max on the bike, his
brother Charlie on
foot, late 1880s.

Max Fleischer at
the *Brooklyn
Daily Eagle,*
1902.

WM. FLEISCHER.

Ladies' Tailor and Importer,
9, 11, 13 East 59th Street.

TELEPHONE CALL, 1920A 79th ST. ....

New York, Jan. 14 1900

My dear Essie,

My letters have been few lately because there was no news to write.

A lady friend of mine is giving a birthday party on Saturday the 19th of this month. (This saturday coming). And has asked me to invite a Brooklyn friend. If you wish to attend let me know by return mail, and I will make arrangements with you. Fanny can come with you if she likes.

My regards to all

Love letter to Essie from Max, 1901, first page.

Hoping you will excuse
my hasty letter I am
Forever Your Friend
Max Fleischer
211 East 57 th St.
New York City.

P.S. Don't fail to write me
before Saturday whether you
can or can not go.
I gaurentee a good time
and the best of company.

Dont disapoint.

Love letter to Essie from Max, 1901, second page.

Lesson no. 1 in "copology": Keep your buttons shiny and William Fleischer happy. (*Brooklyn Daily Eagle* cartoon, 1902, by Max Fleischer.)

Max in the Catskill Mountains near New York City, 1902.

Another *Brooklyn Daily Eagle* cartoon, 1902, by Max Fleischer.

Max's visualization of corruption in Brownsville. (*Brooklyn Daily Eagle* editorial cartoon, 1902, by Max Fleischer.)

Pen-and-ink etching by Max Fleischer.

My father demonstrates for me one of his many inventions, the never-wind clock, at the Windermere Hotel, New York City.

The Rotoscope. Note the living-room drapes and carpet in the Windermere Hotel.

Above: Original tracing of the clown that became known as Ko-Ko. *Below:* Finished artwork based on the tracing.

Ko-Ko the Clown.

A portrait of Max
with a rare relaxed
expression, 1919.

Max posing on a light artillery carriage at Fort Sill, Oklahoma, 1918.

Max with a bayonet at Fort Sill, Oklahoma, 1918.

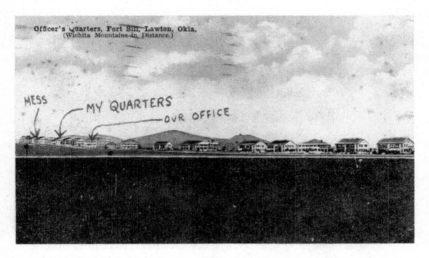

Front side of a postcard sent to daughter, Ruth, 1918.

Back side of a postcard sent to daughter, Ruth, 1918.

Standing next to the camera, Max lines up one of the first U.S. Army training films ever made, Fort Sill, Oklahoma, 1918.

Max and Ko-Ko play together on-screen.

Max and Ko-Ko.

Above: Max Fleischer illustrates the big move from Forty-fifth Street to 1600 Broadway. *Below:* Max participates in a privative special effect.

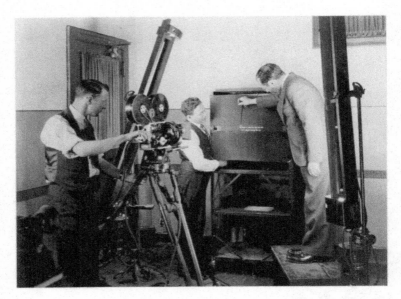

Chas Sheltar, Louis Fleischer, and Max (left to right) prepare a bouncing ball episode.

Max directing Ruth in a scene from *Carrie of the Chorus,* Astoria Studios.

The first of the ill-fated *Carrie of the Chorus* live-action series shooting in Astoria Studios.

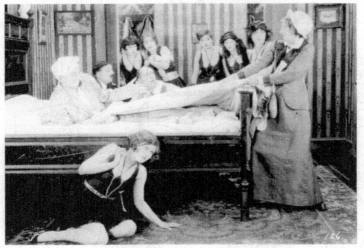

Carrie of the Chorus rehearsal, Ruth third from the right.

Left: The front of one of the first flyers for Betty Boop merchandise. *Below:* The inside of one of the first flyers for Betty Boop merchandise.

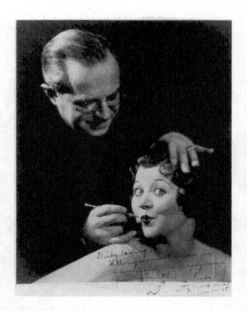

Mae Questel and Max join up to wish me a happy graduation from Peekskill Military Academy into Brown University. Mae writes: "Dicky darling, with my sincerest wishes for a successful and happy career. You deserve it! Love from Betty Boop, alias Mae Questel."

An original drawing of Betty Boop.

The inimitable Mae Questel along with Betty Boop, Bimbo, and Max doing their "selling" act.

Essie (at the left), me (toddler), Ruth (seated), an unknown companion—and the famous Jackson automobile.

Ruth, Max, and I (center) stand next to the Jackson.

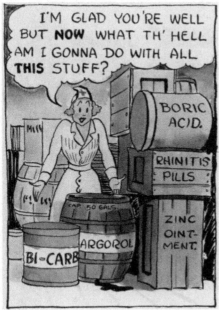

Above and facing page: Get-well cards made for Max by the Fleischer Studios artists.

From The Bowlin' Gals"

Picketers strike Fleischer Studios in New York City, 1937.

Self-caricature by Max Fleischer: an illustration from one of Max's letters on how to spend a pleasant day in New York City in the winter.

Max overlooks the
grounds of his new
home in Miami Beach,
Florida.

A rarity! Max on the
beach, Miami Beach,
Florida.

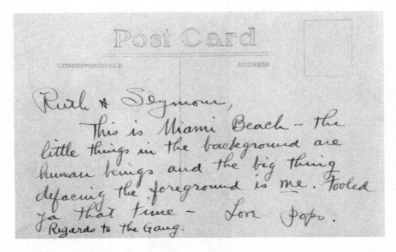

Max writes: "Ruth & Seymour, This is Miami Beach—the little things in the background are human beings and the big thing defacing the foreground is me. Fooled ya that time—Love Pops. Regards to the Gang."

Portrait of Max Fleischer.

Fleischer Studios artists prepare to race their boats in the Florida Everglades.

Max's tummy was expanding, and he enjoyed kidding about it. Max writes: "Your lone BIG POPS, I'm looking in the general direction of my bay window and don't believe the double chin you see, it's a fake! Pops."

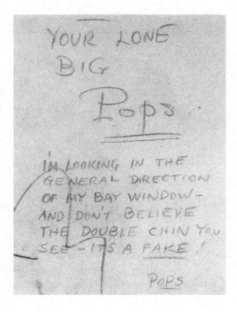

Gulliver's Travels promotional advertisement.

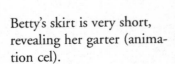

Betty's skirt is very short, revealing her garter (animation cel).

Above and below: Three sketches showing Betty's hemline gradually falling below the knee: "The days of short skirts were going, going, gone."

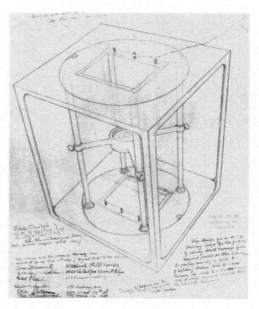

A device used for a double drawing board for the purpose of making direct tracings from original pencil or other drawings, patented 1936.

Superman sketches.

Above: Two Fleischer Studios animation guides.

In a rare moment, Walt Disney and Max enjoy each other's company at Disney Studios, Hollywood, California, 1956.

Inkwell reunion, January 4, 1956.

13

Fleischer Studios prospered. In a couple of years after leaving the tiny, cramped quarters in Long Island City, with a minuscule staff, it occupied four floors at 1600 Broadway with a staff of about 250. New and exciting things were happening in the movie industry. By the mid-1930s, "talkies" had long taken over, and color was creeping in. Max wanted to get into color, but there was a serious case of timidity on Paramount's part. It took the release of Disney's series *Silly Symphonies,* in glorious Technicolor, before Adolph Zukor, the head of Paramount Pictures, green-lighted Fleischer Studios to make a color series.

This new series, *Color Classics,* started out with three strikes against it. First of all, it wasn't the first animated cartoon series to be produced in color. Second, Disney had Technicolor's three-color process tied up with an exclusive contract for cartoon production, so Max couldn't use it. He had to settle instead for the two-strip Cinecolor process. And third, compared to the charming Disney series title *Silly Symphonies, Color Classics* was just plain dull.

Max knew that he had to come up with something special to make his color series stand out and play serious catch-up. First, he decided to do *Poor Cinderella* and cast the leading role with Cartoonland's biggest female star, Betty Boop. And, just to put the cherry on the pie, he convinced Paramount to let him make the picture as a two-reeler instead of the conventional single reel. As far as I know, this was the first two-reel color cartoon ever made. In any event, it was a groundbreaker for feature-length cartoons.

Max took care of the two-strip Cinecolor process by inventing a secret method of using special filters. The end result was that you could hardly tell the difference between Cinecolor and Technicolor. Max's process really was a secret. He didn't want Cinecolor, and especially Technicolor, to know about it. He once heard me mention Cinecolor to someone, took me aside, and, in a conspiratorial manner, whispered never to speak about either company to anyone.

As a final touch, Max decided to use a three-dimensional (3-D) technique that he called the Stereoptical process. He'd been perfecting it for a few years with a brilliant engineer, Johnny Burkes. The idea was to combine real 3-D miniature sets with two-dimensional cartoons. The tiny sets were mounted on a huge turntable that weighed two and a half tons and needed a real Rube Goldberg conglomeration of gears, wheels, pipes, and cranks to operate it. The illusion of depth, however, was uncanny. This apparatus, incidentally, preceded by several years Disney's multiplane camera, which did the same thing. Disney got a lot of credit for creating this new technique. My father got an ulcer.

In spite of the three strikes it had against it, *Poor Cinderella* hit a home run. The glass slipper fit Betty Boop perfectly. Audiences loved the picture, and the theaters treated it like a minifeature, with newspaper reviews and advertising. It even got marquee billing over the regular feature in almost every movie house. No small part of its success was the 3-D effect created by the Stereoptical invention.

The two-reel *Poor Cinderella* was such a hit that Max immediately started work on another two-reel special also using the 3-D effect, *Popeye the Sailor Meets Sinbad the Sailor*. The color in this film was better than ever before since the Disney Technicolor exclusivity was finally at an end and Max was able to use it. The spectacular success of this *Popeye* gave rise to more specials: *Popeye Meets Ali Baba and His Forty Thieves* and *Popeye Meets Aladdin and His Wonderful Lamp*. They were no less successful than the others.

Then reality stepped in. While the use of the 3-D effect in these cartoons added considerably to their popularity, it also added considerably to their budgets. The laborious and painstaking work involved in the use of the turntable, the extra cost of building the miniature sets, the time-consuming and complex photography—it was all just too much for these wonderful cartoons to bear.

Max found himself going down the same path as Disney: acclaimed, award-winning pictures that cost too much money and put the studio in financial jeopardy. He followed his own advice, "You can't eat medals," and, painful though it was, severely limited the use of the 3-D effect.

14

Because of Max and Dave's personalities, Fleischer Studios was a wonderful, happy place to work. Max brought it great paternalistic warmth. He loved the studio and everyone in it, and they loved him back. Dave supplied the fun, the laughter, the devilry. The studio was a place of great camaraderie. Practical jokes were nonstop. The bowling club was extremely popular, and Max never missed an opportunity to play with the gang.

Adding to the general feeling of friendliness was the treatment of all employees, particularly women. In the early 1930s, a time when women in animation studios were limited to the simplest, most menial jobs, with virtually no hope of rising beyond a managerial position, Fleischer Studios employed Lillian Friedman, the first woman animator, and two in-betweeners (assistant animators), Lillian Oremland and Edith Vernick, who later also became an animator.

Another reason for the employees' almost fanatical loyalty

to the studio was also one of the things Max was most proud of: no one ever had to ask for a raise. Every employee automatically received one every six months. Bonuses and prizes were issued every year at the giant Christmas party, to which everyone was invited.

My sister, Ruth, also worked at the studio and, in an interview with Mike Barrier, described it this way: "Nobody ate lunch; we all went to a big room and played poker. That was fun; I liked that. Then we went to Yorkville, the German area in New York; we used to go there to one particular beer garden on Saturday night—Keller's, upstairs—and have the most fantastic parties. When Bill Turner got drunk, the first thing he did was the German dances, with these big German guys."

There was always a feeling of fun and conviviality at the studio. Even getting hospitalized was great sport since the animators always sent handmade get-well cards that were always hilarious—and almost always bawdy.

Ruth says that when she met her future husband, the animator Seymour Kneitel, at the studio, the whole place avidly followed the romance. If she had a date with somebody else, nobody would talk to her the next day. She also points out that, in his office, Dave had a direct wire to the racetrack and a stock-market ticker going all the time. He also kept a bookie in his office, and, what with the animators running in and out all day, it really became a betting parlor. The bookie was the most popular person in the studio.

As far as Max was concerned, what went on outside the business was none of his concern. In fact, he approved of "his kids" whooping it up after work. But what was going on with Dave during business hours was something else. The bookie, the stock ticker, Dave's attitude and behavior, it all began to irritate Max. But, rather than cause friction between them, he didn't make an issue of it.

There was no question about it, however. The studio was one big happy family of almost 250 employees. Or so it seemed.

Talk of unionization had been bandied about the studio for a few years without much interest being stirred. Everyone seemed satisfied with working conditions. Salaries, by the standards of the period, were in keeping with Disney's and the other animation houses.

It was with some surprise, therefore, that in April 1935 all the studio personnel received a pamphlet from an organization calling itself Animated Motion Picture Workers Union. It was, apparently, a fiery document calling for the employees to rise up and take over the studio. It also made a scurrilous attack on Max, blaming him for such poor working conditions, low wages, and long working hours that one employee, Dan Glass, died of tuberculosis as a consequence.

The Dan Glass affair blew over when it was revealed in the monthly studio paper, *Fleischer's Animated News,* that Max had been very concerned about Glass's health and had, among other things, sent him on a week's vacation at a New Jersey resort, all expenses paid. He had also organized a relief fund for financially distressed workers of which Glass was the first beneficiary.

The Animated Motion Picture Workers Union was pretty much of a bust and got exactly nowhere with Fleischer Studios. However, the studio itself was changing. Because of its rapid expansion, the majority of the people working there were newcomers. There was no way that they could have developed the undying loyalty that characterized the upper echelon, most of whom had been with Max and Dave from almost the very beginning. So, like it or not, talk of unionization became a lot more prevalent among the lower-paid, more-or-less-assembly-line employees. Max didn't pay much attention to such talk. He had gotten no complaints, he felt that his people were well treated, and he could see no reason for any kind of outside organization taking a hand in the running of the studio.

The union situation was brought to a boil in July 1935 when the Wagner Labor Relations Act was approved by Congress. Basically, it gave workers the right to organize and make demands of management without any interference from the owners. Not everyone in the studio wanted to make, or could see the need for making, demands of the beloved Max. It was like picking a fight with your father. So a split developed. The family-like atmosphere of the studio began to evaporate.

By 1937, the whole country was awash in strikes, from the United Auto Workers to the Blind Workers' Union. Even Fleischer Studios began to feel the first signs of union fever when a small delegation of employees met with Max to voice some complaints: no paid sick leave; no paid vacations; a forty-five-hour week. Max listened but was unreceptive, probably assuming that this group represented a very small minority of dissatisfied employees.

He figured wrong. A month later, an organization called the Commercial Artists' and Designers' Union (CADU) welcomed over a hundred Fleischer employees into its ranks, and prounion proselytizing began in earnest. It wasn't too long before a CADU delegation met with Max and made a series of what were considered, at the time, outrageous, mind-boggling demands, like double time for overtime and a closed shop.

Max not only refused to negotiate with the union; he refused even to recognize it. He just couldn't believe that most of his employees wanted to join a union. He told the delegation that he didn't believe they represented a majority.

After a series of nonproductive meetings with Max and Louis Nizer, the famous Paramount lawyer, and the union representatives, CADU decided to call a strike for the evening of Friday, May 7, at 6:30 P.M. The reason for that hour was because the studio had changed its schedule of working a half day on Saturday mornings to working three and a half hours on Friday evenings. Both sides were confident that the strike would be settled quickly.

The evening started with a lighthearted sense of humor. The picket signs were mostly meant to be funny: "We can't get much spinach on salaries as low as $15"; and "I make millions laugh but the real joke is our salaries." The jollity lasted until about five of the nonstrikers came back from dinner and found the building entrance blocked by the circling pickets happily singing: "I'm Popeye the Union Man." They decided to cross the line and force their way in. That's when the picket signs became not so funny.

A fight started. Signs were swung. Charlie Schettler, head of the Camera Department, got his nose broken by one of them. Seymour Kneitel got a split lip from a punch in the mouth; another animator was beaten up by one of the pickets who had worked under him. The cops arrived and started manhandling the strikers. It turned into a proper brawl—a melee, in fact. It lasted about half an hour and attracted a crowd of two thousand New Yorkers. And the press, of course, gave it proper coverage the next morning. The *New York Daily News* carried a headline: "POPEYE AND BETTY BOOP JOIN FILM STRIKE HERE."

Max was truly shocked by the intensity of the strikers' emotions. He was both angry and dismayed that so many of his people weren't totally loyal to him and the studio. He couldn't understand the violence. There were frequent scuffles on the picket line at the studio entrance. Strikers were picketing in front of the Windermere Hotel, where Max lived, and in front of Dave's house as well. They invaded some theaters that were running Fleischer cartoons, particularly the Paramount Theatre and the Roxy, booing and hissing, yelling for the picture to be taken off.

Meetings between the studio and CADU were held intermittently, with no result. Max refused to recognize the union as a legitimate bargaining agent. All the entertainment guilds and unions were solidly lined up against the studio, which made for a peculiar situation for Dave and Lou Fleischer, who were members of the American Federation of Musicians, which was supporting the strike. Dave and Lou could end up having to picket themselves.

The strike dragged on for about six months, and toward the end some of the strikers were running out of steam and money. More and more of them started to drift back into the studio. By the time an agreement was reached between the studio and CADU, the strike had just about petered out. The strikers actually got pretty much everything they'd wanted, just scaled way back from their original demands.

Max never recognized the union, and the studio never became a closed shop. Anyone could work for the studio without becoming a CADU member. The wounds from the strike would take a long time to heal.

15

Max was a dyed-in-the-wool New Yorker. He rarely traveled outside the city. His out-of-the-country experience, not counting his first four years in Austria, amounted to three days in Canada and one night in Mexico. He didn't do much better within the United States. New York City was his home, and almost nothing could lure him away from it—except Miami Beach. He liked Miami Beach so much that, in 1933, he actually bought a winter home there. It was a modest two-story, Spanish-style house at 3090 Alton Road for which he paid $31,500.

During the nasty strike business, Max started to become disillusioned with New York, and his thoughts turned more and more to the attractions of his home in Miami Beach. He often dreamed about building from scratch a state-of-the-art animated cartoon studio there.

Then, on December 21, 1937, a world-shattering event took place in the motion picture industry. Walt Disney premiered

Snow White and the Seven Dwarfs. It was the first feature-length Technicolor cartoon, and to call it a phenomenal success would be a vast understatement. For several years, Max had wanted to make a feature-length cartoon, but Adolph Zukor, the head of Paramount Pictures, had always turned him down. Who wants to sit through such a long cartoon? It would be too expensive. It would take too long to make.

Apparently, Mr. Zukor's cloudy crystal ball suddenly cleared up because Max was informed that Paramount wanted a feature-length color cartoon. Naturally, Max and Dave were overjoyed, but the problems facing them were nothing less than daunting. Their present staff was about 250. In order to make a feature and still keep up their present output of short cartoons, they would have to expand to seven hundred or more.

Obviously, their present quarters at 1600 Broadway were far too small to house that number of artists and technicians. Any space in and around New York large enough to accommodate a mob like that would be prohibitively expensive. And, with a mob like that, union problems were inevitable. It made Max shudder even to consider that prospect.

Then, one night at home in the Windermere, Max mentioned these problems to Essie. "Why don't you talk to the councilmen down in Miami?" she asked. "Maybe they can help." Max was puzzled by the suggestion. Then he remembered that Essie, being the wife of an international celebrity, had been introduced to some of the city councilmen at a charity dinner in Miami. They had told her how proud they were to have Max buying a home there and had dropped some serious hints about his moving the studio to Miami. They could make it very attractive, they said. Essie had mentioned this conversation to

Max when she got back to New York from a short vacation. It was such a far-fetched notion that, at the time, Max had given it no consideration whatsoever.

But suddenly it wasn't such a far-fetched notion at all. In fact, two days later Max was in a special meeting of the city council members in Miami. In order to understand what was happening, it is necessary to remember that Miami then was not Miami now. In the late 1930s, Miami and Miami Beach were underpopulated, underbuilt, and underknown (the Flagler House was the only large hotel in Miami Beach). The city was desperately looking for someone or something to put it on the map and boost its economy. With Max and a movie studio the equal of Disney's, plus hundreds of new residents coming in, Miami could have it all.

The city councilmen presented Max with a sweetheart deal if ever there was one. There was no space large enough or suitable enough to take care of the studio's personnel. But, if Max wanted to build a new studio from scratch, they would practically give him all the land he needed. Special deals would be worked out for construction costs. The new studio would be exempt from some taxes and have others drastically reduced with long deferments for payment. Anything and everything that was needed to get the studio built in Miami would be provided on the most favorable terms possible.

And then there was the most attractive element of all. Florida was a nonunion state. Unions were weak or nonexistent. There would be no union problems. Guaranteed!

It looked like Essie had once again come to the rescue of one of Max's "crazy ideas," just as she had many years before when he was developing the Rotoscope.

It took unimaginable vision and courage, and more than a little insanity, to do what Max had in mind. For one thing, he was proposing building a thirty-two-thousand-square-foot studio loaded with state-of-the-art equipment in every branch of motion picture and animated cartoon production. For another, he was asking all his New York employees to move to Miami and, to encourage them to do so, offering to move their families and close relatives (grandparents, stepparents, in-laws, etc.) as well, all expenses paid. He would provide temporary housing for them; he would ship their furniture; he would even move them back to New York if, after a year, they wanted to leave Miami. About 250 employees took him up on the offer. But, even with the influx of New York employees, there were not enough trained artists in Miami to fully staff the studio. So Max planned to open two free animation-oriented drawing schools and guarantee studio jobs to anyone who satisfactorily completed the course.

This would be a very expensive venture. The building alone would cost well over $300,000. But, compared to rents and other costs of doing business in New York, it was feasible. It would be something akin to Moses leading the Israelites out of Egypt, but it was feasible.

Instead of going to a bank, as Disney had done when he needed money, Max presented the whole plan to Paramount. The company found it attractive enough that it agreed to loan Fleischer Studios the funds to finance the entire project. On May 27, 1938, in the offices of Fleischer Studios at 1600 Broadway, using the entire library of already-produced cartoons as collateral, Max signed a deal with Paramount ratifying the loan. It was a monumental, tragic mistake.

16

Work at the New York studio continued at full force on the *Betty Boops,* the *Popeyes,* and other shorts during the five or so months it took to build the Florida studio. The greatest concentration, however, was given to deciding what story to use for the feature. I wasn't at all surprised when Jonathan Swift's *Gulliver's Travels* was chosen. I knew it was my father's favorite book since he used to read it to me as a bedtime story when I was a child. The section chosen, dealing with the Lilliputians, was certainly the most popular and the best suited to an animated cartoon treatment. For a while the idea of having Popeye play Gulliver got kicked around, but it was eventually decided to leave well enough alone. I can't help thinking, however, that Popeye as Gulliver would have been intriguing.

The new Florida studio seemed to appear out of thin air, as though a magician had reversed the wording of his usual patter and announced: "Now you don't see it . . . now you do!" Just five months earlier, only stunted palmettos and sandy scrub stood at NW Thirtieth Avenue and Seventeenth Street in Miami. Now there appeared a pristine one-story white concrete building, a city block square, with a brand-new hundred-foot-wide boulevard running past its entrance. It was the new Fleischer Studios, the most advanced animation studio in the world.

The new studio was the first completely air-conditioned building in Florida. Its sound-recording stage and mixing equipment were state-of-the-art, as were its fifty-seat theater and projection system. Every detail, from the cafeteria to the machine shop, was impeccably designed and built.

Building contractors soon had the empty area around the studio dotted with cheap, small, jerry-built houses. The whole migration was, in itself, an interesting sociological event. Being away at Brown University in Rhode Island, I barely saw the impact on those who made the move.

My sister, Ruth, and her husband, Seymour Kneitel, however, were very much a part of the exodus. Ruth made these observations in a Mike Barrier interview: "Half of them [the New York employees] got down there and their wives hated it, and a lot of them packed up and went back. Out of that half that went back, more than half came back after the first winter."

Many of the studio people moved into the small, newly built houses that were near the studio, but most families found it more convenient to live in town, closer to the city of Miami. Property in Miami Beach was always expensive. Few studio people came to the beach. Dave bought a house there.

My mother and father bought what can only be described as an estate, on the Biscayne Bay side of Miami Beach, at 2324 North Bay Road. It was a spacious house with many large, high-ceilinged rooms. In fact, the master bedroom had a concert grand piano in one corner that didn't look out of place at all.

The house itself stood on two beautifully landscaped lots and also boasted a small pier jutting out into the flat-calm Biscayne Bay waters. We gave up fishing from the pier after we caught several truly disgusting-looking tropical fish with huge, razor-sharp teeth and powerful jaws to snap them with. You couldn't even think of unhooking them if you valued any of your fingers. They seemed to be the only fish we could catch.

However, the pier was a great place to stand and wave when tourist boats passed by, singling out, over amplified loudspeakers, the homes of the rich and famous. The residence of Max Fleischer was always pointed out. My mother had picked up the English-royalty wave from one of our European trips and would always come running to the pier when she heard a boat approaching, trying to wave as queenly as possible.

My father had other uses for the pier. He was bent on constructing a clock that could be kept wound by the movement of the tides and the action of the waves. There couldn't be a less ideal place to accomplish this than Biscayne Bay, which had a tide of about six inches and no waves at all except for the intermittent ripples created by the occasional slow-moving boats. He converted part of the four-car garage into a workshop, where he worked for countless weekend hours on his never-wind clock. What he was really striving for was a way of harnessing an endless supply of energy from the sea.

Max finally perfected and, I believe, patented the never-wind clock. He mounted it on the pier, where it remained for a year or so, accurately keeping the time, before corrosion took its toll and it finally fell into the bay.

Until they could find a house they liked in Miami Beach, Ruth, Seymour, and their small family moved into the big house with our folks. I was on one of my school breaks and was also staying there. As large as the house was, space was getting a bit tight, particularly closet space. Even the large closet in my father's dressing room seemed cramped. Max never paid much attention to what he wore, so Essie would sometimes buy clothes for him and have them altered later, when he had time for a fitting.

One morning he discovered a couple of jackets and some slacks in the closet that didn't look familiar, but that wasn't unusual. He tried them on, and nothing fit well at all, so he took them with him to the studio and had the seamstress alter them. A couple of weeks later, Seymour went into my father's dressing room and came out looking like a scarecrow, with his trousers well above his ankles, his sleeves well above his wrists, and one hand clutching a wad of loose fabric at the belt line. It seems that Seymour had temporarily stored some of his clothes in my father's closet and Max had had them altered.

17

Paramount insisted on a Christmas release date for *Gulliver's Travels,* which was fine, except that it had to be Christmas of 1939, which was a year and a half away. *Snow White* took four years to make, so the challenge was intimidating, to say the least.

The studio started hiring artists like mad. Besides the 250 from New York, at least 100 were hired from among local artists, another 300 from the training schools that had been set up, and about 100 from West Coast studios like Disney's or Walter Lantz's or wherever they could be found. (Walter Lantz was the creator of, among other characters, Woody Woodpecker and Chilly Willy.) The once-spacious studio was soon jammed with 760 employees. Some units had to work in nearby hired space.

It is interesting to see how Max's inventive mind worked in this situation. In order to speed up production without making impossible demands on the artists, he looked for a mechanical solution. One of the most time-consuming processes in animation work is what is known as *inking,* when the pencil-drawn lines made by the animators are extremely carefully traced in ink onto a cel. It is a slow, meticulous, tedious job.

Max wanted to get rid of the Inking Department altogether. So this man, who had never taken a course in chemistry, set up a laboratory in the studio and started experimenting. He developed a new kind of pencil that, instead of lead, contained his secret formula. If the animator drew with that special pencil, those lines could be transferred to a cel mechanically by the use of a special press, which Max also designed. Inking would be completely bypassed.

It almost worked, but not quite. Or, as the saying goes, it was close, but no cigar. The lines came out too fat, or too thin, or too smeary. After about six months of experimentation, Max reluctantly abandoned the project. Eventually, the Xerox Corporation came out with a similar method of transferring pencil to cel that is used by many studios today. It seems that Max almost invented Xeroxing.

Incredibly, *Gulliver* came in on schedule. Its premiere in Miami Beach on December 18, 1939, was an event so eagerly anticipated that the Sheridan Theatre, where it was scheduled to open, was completely sold out the week before and a second theater, the Colony, was booked for a simultaneous showing.

Reviews were, for the most part, excellent, with a substantial number of raves. Naturally, there were comparisons with *Snow White.* These were not as invidious as might be expected. The *Boston Traveler* commented: "*Gulliver's Travels* has much of the delightful charm and humor of *Snow White* and should be much more entertaining than the Disney classic." Very few, if any, reviewers made one important comparison between the two films: *Snow White* cost $3.5 million to make, while *Gulliver's Travels* came in at $1 million.

The picture did tremendous business, breaking house records everywhere. Every screening at the Paramount Theatre in New York was completely sold out. People waited for the next showing in freezing temperatures and in lines three and four deep that went clear around the corner. For the first time in its history, the theater instituted an 8:30 A.M. showing, keeping it for the entire run of the film.

I've often read that *Gulliver* was not a commercial success. This is not true. Despite the concurrent outbreak of war in Europe and the resulting loss of foreign income, the picture did so well that Paramount immediately ordered a second animated feature, *Mr. Bug Goes to Town.*

Now, with the studio in high gear as well as high overhead, Max decided to put it into overdrive. Although good old Popeye the Sailor was as popular and profitable as ever, new product was needed to keep all those hundreds of employees busy. Unfortunately, Betty Boop couldn't be called on to help out. Her series had finally been discontinued after she ran afoul of the Motion Picture Production Code, adopted in 1930 by the Motion Picture Association of America to censor smut and indecency in motion pictures. The Production Code was aimed primarily at Mae West, but its scattershot approach didn't exempt cartoons. The harmless but mildly provocative Betty Boop became a target of the overzealous Production Code people.

If it weren't so tragic, it would be laughable. Fleischer Studios was hounded and even threatened until Betty started to change. Just as she changed at the beginning of her career from a dog to a person, she now had to change from a mini-sexpot to a sort of schoolmarm. First, her garter was taken away; next, the hemline on her very short skirt was lowered; finally, her neckline was raised. All the fun and spice had been taken out of Betty Boop, and, through no fault of her own, her popularity waned. It broke Max's heart when he finally had to discontinue his beloved *Betty Boop* series.

To keep the studio humming, various ideas for new series were tried. A whole flock of cute figures had been featured in *Gulliver's Travels*—Gabby, Twinkletoes, Sneak, Snoop, Snitch, and others. A series of shorts was made featuring these characters, as were some two-reelers like *Raggedy Ann* and *Raggedy Andy,* but none of them seemed to catch on. The studio even made a series called *Stone Age Cartoons* in which the characters built various machines and devices out of Stone Age materials. These cartoons were quite a novelty, having predated *The Flintstones* by a good twenty years, but they never gained the popularity needed to carry them for more than a year.

However, all that changed when Paramount approached Max and Dave with the idea of making an animated cartoon series about Superman, a wildly popular Action Comics character created by Jerry Siegel and Joe Schuster. The Fleischers had some trepidation about jumping into this project since the *Superman* comics had a distinctive style. The characters were very realistically drawn human beings, and the compositions in each panel were well designed and dramatically composed.

To turn *Superman* into an animated cartoon would take a lot more time, skill, and effort than went into the average short cartoon. And it would be a lot more expensive. At the risk of losing the project, the Fleischer brothers were forthright with

Paramount. The average cartoon, they told the studio, costs about $50,000 per reel. *Superman* would cost $100,000 per reel. They thought that would be the end of the project—but it wasn't. Paramount said: "Okay, go ahead."

The success of the series was beyond anyone's expectations. The *Superman* cartoons still rank among the best cartoons ever put on the screen. This time everything clicked for the Fleischers, even the music and the slogan they contributed: "Look! Up in the sky . . . It's a bird! It's a plane! It's Superman!" That slogan swept the world and, like other Fleischer creations, became a permanent part of our culture.

18

The studio's move from New York to Miami was an apparent success; the *Popeye* and *Superman* series were going great guns; *Gulliver's Travels* was breaking attendance records at box offices everywhere while another feature-length cartoon, *Mr. Bug Goes to Town*, was in preparation; and, to top it all, the *Screen Songs* series, with the bouncing ball, was an unexpected hit. Things at the new Miami studio were humming right along without a hitch.

Well, almost without a hitch. According to Max's notes, he and Dave were not getting along—in fact, they weren't even talking to each other. Dave's playboy attitude that had irked Max in New York hadn't changed. If anything, it was getting more irksome. The New York bookie, not wanting to lose his clientele, had moved to Miami too. Once again, Dave's office became a betting parlor, with a bookie, a direct wire to the track, and a ticker. The gang that frequented Dave's office would take the bookie out to dinner on Saturday nights. That really annoyed Max.

Miami Beach was a wide-open town. Some pretty lavish illegal gaming casinos had sprung up, and Dave was a frequent customer. Max enjoyed some of the gambling—those games for which you could try to figure the odds—but he rarely went. Essie, of course, was in heaven.

But it wasn't the gambling so much as it was Dave's profligate, reckless lifestyle that got under Max's skin. And the brothers' relationship got put on the fast track to destruction when Dave left his wife and family and openly took up with his secretary, May Schwartz. Although he was liberal in most ways, Max had a strong, truly Victorian attitude when it came to morality. This business with Dave offended him deeply. When Dave started to take May to the track during the working week, Max's annoyance turned to anger. As far as he was concerned, Dave's behavior was unforgivable.

This situation was starting to put Ruth and me in an uncomfortable position. The problem was that we loved Dave and he was genuinely fond of us. He had a wonderful sense of humor and was great fun to be with. We asked Max if it bothered him when Dave would hire a pleasure boat and invite Ruth, Seymour, and me to go fishing with him in the Everglades. Max always pooh-poohed the idea that he might be offended, but if he had been, he would never have let his children know.

Dave's lifestyle was a constant irritant to Max. He believed that Dave's mind was much too devoted to gambling, the stock market, and the horses. The fact that these pastimes were carried out during business hours gave rise to occasional confrontations, during which, according to Max, Dave became abusive and unreasonable. There was also a growing irritation on Dave's part that Max was getting more publicity than he was, and there were confrontations about that, too.

The real break between the brothers, however, seems to have come out of left field. During the preproduction period of *Gulliver's Travels,* Max came up with the idea of using Robin and Rainger, a top Hollywood songwriting team with many hits and movie credits ("Thanks for the Memory," "Love in Bloom"). Getting them to write the score would be a real coup. Max presented the idea to Dave, who dismissed it out of hand. He had a much better idea—he would write the music and lyrics himself!

Max was incredulous. In all the years Dave had been in close contact with the studio's Music Department, he had never come up with a single theme, much less a whole score. Max couldn't see putting the musical fate of this highly important project in the hands of an untested novice. But Dave was insistent. He argued that they didn't need Robin and Rainger, that he could do it just as well.

Max notified Paramount of his and Dave's difference of opinion about the music. Paramount agreed that Max was right and also approved the use of the songwriting team to score the film. Max immediately signed Robin and Rainger.

Dave was furious. He couldn't be appeased or reasoned with. From that moment on, he refused to speak to Max on either personal or business matters. As it says in the Bible: "A brother offended is harder to be won than a strong city: and their contentions are like the bars of a castle" (Prov. 18:19). Truer words were never writ.

On May 2, 1940, a special meeting was held in the Miami

studio with Max, Dave, and the corporation's longtime lawyer, N. William Welling. It was basically agreed that the affairs of the company would be divided into business and production, with Max in charge of the business end and Dave the production. In his own sphere, each would have the final decision. However, each had the right to offer suggestions and ideas to the other.

The enmity between the brothers was such that they would not talk to each other. If communication were necessary, the special meeting decreed, it would be in writing, and the recipient would acknowledge that communication in writing.

The situation didn't improve any when the time came to select a composer for *Mr. Bug Goes to Town*. Max's choice was the legendary Hoagy Carmichael, the songwriter responsible for such great standards as "Stardust" and "Georgia on My Mind," and Frank Loesser, who had such hits as *Guys and Dolls* and *How to Succeed in Business without Really Trying*. Dave's choice was, once again, himself. Carmichael and Loesser did the picture.

Running a major animated cartoon studio solely by written communiqué turned out to be a sort of tragicomedy. In a lengthy memo sent to Dave dated October 8, 1940, Max analyzes the screenplay of *Mr. Bug Goes to Town* in great, and valid, detail. For every criticism he made, he included a reasonable, well-thought-out solution. The tone of the memo was completely professional. It was the kind of memo any reasonable director would welcome.

On October 16, Dave replied with this rather stiff memo:

Max:
    I received your communication of October 8th, and wish to advise you that I have read its contents very

carefully. Since the story is now quite complete and all ready for animation it is quite late for any real changes. However, I will consider your suggestions carefully as I again go through the story.

Dave

The letter is really a "thank-you for the suggestions, but no thank-you" letter. Max, however, was apparently willing to try to loosen things up. On December 2, 1940, he sent this memo to Dave: "The two reeler, Raggedy Ann is an admirable piece of work and probably the best cartoon made in our Studios in some time. The result as a whole, is entirely satisfactory and deserving of comment." There was no acknowledgment from Dave.

By March 1940, the situation was getting testier, and Max was getting more pointed in his innuendos. In a memo to Dave on March 26, he critiqued several items in an unfinished short. At the end of his memo, he wrote: "If you are too busy to give this picture several days of your personal attention, let me know and I will consult with the cutters and editors assigned to the film."

The odd thing about this whole situation was that it didn't interfere with the running of the studio at all. Work on *Mr. Bug* was going smoothly and according to plan; the *Popeye, Superman,* and bouncing ball *Screen Songs* series, as well as all the numerous other cartoons, were completed on schedule and on budget. There were no criticisms or complaints from Paramount whatsoever. It was a calm sea with a fair wind despite the subsurface tensions. Until May 29, 1941.

19

On May 29, 1941, Dick Murray, the liaison man between Fleischer Studios and Paramount in New York, arrived at the studio in Miami and handed Max a large manila envelope. It contained a sixty-five-page, closely typed contract, dated May 24, between Paramount and Fleischer Studios. Max was completely puzzled. It was a contract he had never seen or heard of before. Murray told him to read it as soon as he could. Max opened the contract, read the first paragraph, and was completely stunned. It stated: "All understandings and agreements, of whatever nature (between Paramount and Fleischer Studios), shall be, and are hereby, terminated and canceled as of May 24, 1941, and Paramount shall have no further obligation to make any payments whatsoever."

As near as he could recall, Max reports that the following conversation with Dick Murray took place:

Max [*after reading first paragraph*]: What does this mean?

Murray: All I know is that you are to read it and sign.

Max: The first paragraph is shocking. Who wrote this?

Murray: I don't know.

Max: Have you read this contract?

Murray: No, I didn't read it.

Max: Did Lou Phillips [a Paramount lawyer] hand it to you for delivery?

Murray: Lou is out of town, and I'm not authorized to say who handed the contract to me. Why don't you read it through?

Max: You surprise me, Dick. The whole story is in the first paragraph. Didn't you even read that?

Murray: All I can say is, they want me to bring the contract back signed . . . this week, or else.

Max: By *or else,* do they mean bankruptcy?

Murray: You can take it that way, but you better get it signed, otherwise the next payroll won't come through.

Max: Do you mean to tell me that Paramount won't even give me enough time to secure another distributor?

Murray: Definitely not.

Max was in shock as he sat down to read the rest of the contract, a contract unilaterally drawn, without consultation with or even the knowledge of the other party. If that first paragraph was brutal, what followed was crushing. That first paragraph killed the studio; the rest of the document stripped the corpse.

The contract demanded that all assets, including patents, trademarks, and copyrights, be turned over to Paramount. Now, fourteen of the copyrights and patents were personally owned by Max and were never assigned to Fleischer Studios. He permitted the use of them so long as he was connected with the studio. This new contract demanded that these be turned over to Paramount, together with every other asset of the company, including all its intellectual property rights, personal property, and real property subject to any subordination agreements.

In order to finance the move from New York to Miami, Fleischer Studios had indebted itself to Paramount. Under the 1938 agreement, Fleischer could amortize that loan over a ten-year period. Now Paramount was demanding payment after only three years.

But there was still the final blow to come. Fleischer Studios would cease to exist at the end of business on May 23 and re-open as Famous Studios on May 24.

It was truly a Kafkaesque situation. The sudden destruction of his beloved studio, a lifetime of work and dreams, gone. And for no reason, not a single word in the contract giving a clue as to why it happened.

Max immediately phoned N. William Welling, his New York lawyer, and explained the situation to him. Welling didn't seem surprised by the news. His response was even more shocking to Max than the contract itself. Welling advised Max to sign the papers to avoid the disgrace of missing a payroll, saying: "We can take care of that matter later on and have the ownership returned to you."

Bankruptcy to Max was anathema. In the 1940s, it was something to be avoided at all costs. It carried the stigma of failure and shame. Bankruptcy then was not what it is today, a refuge, a place of comfort to hide from creditors. For Max, bankruptcy was unthinkable.

And there were the studio's employees, all 760 of them, to consider. Max felt a great personal responsibility toward them, particularly the 250 who had put their trust in him and followed him to Miami with their families and household goods.

Max was faced with a huge, soul-wrenching dilemma: sign the contract, and give away the studio to Paramount; or refuse to sign, and let Paramount withhold the studio's payroll and force him into bankruptcy. There were only a few days left before the payroll was due.

His thoughts, which he later committed to paper, ran something like this: In a bankruptcy, all his patents and film assets would eventually be placed on public auction. He would be obliged to bid against Paramount. This would be impossible. He would never stand a chance in a bidding contest with a giant like Paramount.

On the other hand, signing would give him time and an opportunity to figure out exactly what was behind Paramount's sudden and unwarranted move. The new contract included for both Max and Dave a twenty-six-week term of employment commencing May 24.

The studio was still committed to making twelve more *Popeyes,* twelve more *Superman* shorts, and several two-reel cartoons as well as completing *Mr. Bug Goes to Town.* Max and Dave were needed to run the studio in order for Paramount to meet its picture commitments. However, each had to sign a letter of resignation to be kept until Paramount asked for it.

Max's final reasoning came down to this: If I sign, I will

walk out without the stigma of bankruptcy. If I don't sign, I will walk out of the entire industry with an everlasting bankruptcy reputation. My best move is to sign and walk out clean.

He sent the contract to Dave, with a note attached, telling him to sign. It was another shock for Max when the sixty-five-page contract, signed by Dave, came back to him in less than five minutes! Obviously, Dave had signed it without reading it. He wondered why. Had Dave already seen the contract? Something strange and sinister was afoot, but Max couldn't yet figure out what it was. He signed the contract.

On the next business day, Max and Dave Fleischer went to work as employees of Famous Studios. Their humiliation was complete.

20

After the initial shock of the Paramount takeover, things at Famous Studios went on much as they had at Fleischer Studios. The films were still being released under the Fleischer Studios' banner. The name change would not be made public until May 1943, when the whole operation was to be moved back to 1600 Broadway in New York.

In the meantime, although the brothers were still not talking, production went smoothly. Films were completed on schedule and on budget, and the feature film *Mr. Bug Goes to Town* was nearing completion. Max and Dave put their best efforts into the studio's program in order to protect their reputations for producing first-class animated product that carried their name.

Max assumed that, once he instituted a lawsuit, Paramount would claim that, because of the brothers' feuding, the studio was falling apart, operating inefficiently, and had to be taken over. Paramount had no other conceivable reason, or complaint, for taking the action it had. He didn't want to give the company even a shaky leg to stand on.

In order to ensure the highest quality possible, Dave took the final edit of *Mr. Bug* to Hollywood for music recording. He must have made some good contacts while he was there because, on November 22, 1941, he mailed in his resignation to the studio and never returned. (In later years, he ran the Columbia Pictures cartoon studio and, later still, became a general factotum at Universal Studios, watching over and making suggestions about various projects in production.)

It was Cervantes who said: "Ill luck, you know, seldom comes alone." Max's ill luck came with a mob scene. First, there was the mild, but truly unfortunate, heart attack suffered by his son-in-law (Ruth's husband), Seymour Kneitel, in late March 1941. Seymour was one of the studio's very top animators and a wonderful guy. I considered him my brother rather than my brother-in-law. However, while the heart attack was mild, its psychological consequences were long-lasting and unexpectedly and unpredictably serious. Next, in mid-May, the Paramount bombshell exploded. Then, three days before the release of *Mr. Bug Goes to Town,* so did another bombshell: the Japanese attack at Pearl Harbor. Audiences were not in the mood to see an amusing animated cartoon feature, so *Mr. Bug* bombed too.

Still, the final blow, the unkindest cut, was yet to come. Barney Balaban, the president of Paramount Pictures, called for a meeting with Max at the New York office on December 28. Max arrived on time and was taken to a conference room where Balaban and four or five other executives awaited him. After the usual formalities, Balaban motioned to a vacant chair. Max sat, wondering what it could be that had brought him on a long, overnight train trip from Miami to this large paneled room in a New York skyscraper. The answer wasn't long in coming.

According to Max's written report of that meeting, Balaban said: "Max, we have decided to accept your resignation." Feeling nothing but numbness, Max responded: "This is all very puzzling. What is the purpose of all this?" Balaban replied: "That's our decision." End of meeting.

It was pure *Alice in Wonderland.* Max asks a peculiar question, and Balaban gives a peculiar nonanswer. Fourteen years of a smooth, friendly, nonconfrontational relationship had come to an abrupt and puzzling end. Max returned to Miami to close his affairs at the studio he had built, sell the house, and wonder why it all happened. His question to Balaban at the New York meeting, "What is the purpose of all this?" was a good one. It was a question that he kept asking himself, but the answer remained a tormenting, gut-torturing mystery.

Shortly after he resigned from Famous Studios, Max—who had moved back to New York—had a meeting with the Paramount Legal Department there. He had much to discuss with them. At that time in motion picture history, major studios owned hundreds of theaters through which they released their films, a practice that was eventually found illegal and banned by law. Such an arrangement allowed the studios to keep accurate tabs on the income reported by each individual theater. Paramount owned, in whole or in part, about fourteen hundred theaters. Each theater was charged a fee for the showing of a cartoon, a fee that was supposed to be shared with Fleischer Studios. Knowing the production cost of each cartoon, Paramount charged each theater just enough so that Fleischer Studios' share of the aggregate either just covered, or was less than, the cost of making the cartoon. Paramount then shared the actual excess profits with the theaters. At least this was what Max was convinced Paramount was doing. No accounting was ever made to Fleischer Studios.

At the meeting, Max didn't bring up this accounting technique directly, just danced around it. All present knew what he was referring to. But his main topic was the matter of patent ownership. The infamous 1941 contract included several patents that were Max's personal property, such as the highly valuable Rear Screen (or Rear View) Projection patent, otherwise known as Process photography or the Process shot. And Max pointed out that Paramount's own records were enough to win his case for him. As he put it: "No sane man would turn over to Paramount his patent ownership shortly before leaving his own company unless . . ." Lou Phillips, one of the lawyers and a Paramount vice president, asked: "Unless what?" "Unless duress was introduced," Max replied. "Now," he went on, "what inducement would a man have to give up his ownership of patents when he was preparing to leave his own company?" The meeting was promptly terminated.

Between 4:45 P.M., when the meeting broke up, and 5:30 P.M., when Max arrived home, Phillips had contacted Max's son-in-law, Seymour Kneitel, recently recovered from a heart attack and now in charge of Paramount's Famous Studios, the former Fleischer Studios. Phillips told Seymour that Max had visited Paramount, that the matters that Max had brought up were of a serious nature, and that, if Max carried things further, Seymour would be seriously affected.

For Max, this clear and present threat to the well-being of Seymour's family (like Seymour getting fired) was intolerable;

the possibility that Seymour's family would suffer, unthinkable. Seymour and Ruth did their best to persuade him otherwise, but he was stubborn. He was convinced that Paramount's threat was made to stop him from pressing on with his accusations in a court of law.

It worked. The threat stopped him.

21

Almost before the news of the studio's sudden demise had had a chance to travel, Max was paid a visit in Miami by an old friend and alumnus of the J. R. Bray days, Jamison Handy. Max and Handy had been good friends in those early days, and now Handy was offering a helping hand to his old friend Max. Handy was based in Detroit as the president of the Jam Handy Organization, an outfit that made educational and army training films and maintained a small animation department.

First, he asked if there was any way in which he could intervene with Balaban on Max's behalf. Max told him that it was all over and that he could see no chance of anyone doing any good. Handy then asked Max whether he could move to Detroit and assist his organization in the production of military training films for the government. Since Max had made the very first training films during World War I, he seemed a natural candidate for making them and updating them during World War II.

Another part of the deal was for him to continue making special animated shorts and to invent, develop, and improve whatever he wished to involve himself with.

The offer couldn't have come at a more fortuitous moment. It was more than a distraction to keep the present disaster from being overwhelming; it was something to look forward to. It was the kind of work Max loved, a combination of science, mechanics, and illustrative art. It was also part of the war effort. Plus Max was joining an organization that appreciated and honored him. It was a deal. Max and Jam Handy shook on it.

At just about the time Max and Essie were moving into an apartment in the Seward Hotel in Detroit, the former Fleischer Studios was in the process of being moved back to 1600 Broadway in New York City. Paramount had cut the staff and salaries pretty drastically and had selected three people to run the new Famous Studios: Seymour Kneitel to be in charge and run the studio; longtime employee Sam Buchwald to act as studio manager; and Izzy Sparber, who had been with the studio from virtually day one, to serve as studio accountant.

Paramount's choice of Seymour as the new boss may have been a lot shrewder than it appeared. For one thing, he was the only animator among the three and creatively brilliant. Just as important, however, it might have been an insurance policy of sorts. Who knew what would happen if Seymour, recently recovered from a heart attack, with a wife and three small children and the stress of moving the studio and his family back to New York, suddenly found himself on the job market?

Max was supremely aware of this scenario. He wouldn't even discuss a lawsuit under these circumstances. His nightmare, he told me more than once, was exactly what Paramount may have had in mind. Max was determined to wait until things stabilized. There was no way that he would do anything to endanger Seymour and his family. A lawsuit could wait. There was time.

Shortly after moving to Detroit, Max contacted Famous Studios, requesting that all his papers and files be sent to him. He knew that he would have to rely on them heavily once he got a lawsuit started, and he wanted to be well prepared. It was with shocked incomprehension that he received the news that all his records, files, and books, personal and otherwise, had disappeared, leaving behind not a trace. It was another stunning blow.

To make matters even worse, Max was notified that his federal tax return was being audited. During the audit, he was asked to explain certain figures, but, without his papers and files, he was unable to do that. His "lost records" explanation was not kindly received, even though he offered to state the facts in affidavit form.

The Tax Bureau and the FBI conducted a thorough investigation of Max and Paramount. Finally, they became convinced that, even with Paramount's disclaimer of any knowledge about the existence of Max's records, his figures were correct.

This was all well and good, but what had happened to the papers? If the feds couldn't find them, who could? Max desperately needed those papers. The only one who might be able to get to the bottom of this matter would be his personal secretary, Vera Coleman.

If ever there was a perfect secretary, Vera was it. She had been Max's personal secretary for at least twenty years and was totally and irrevocably devoted to him. She knew everything there was to know about his private and public life, the studio, what he liked and disliked, how he thought. She knew him inside out, backwards and sideways, so much so that she chose to follow "the boss" to Detroit and remain his secretary. Even I depended on her totally. After all, she was the one who sent me my allowance every week when I was away at school. If anyone could find out what had happened to the papers, it would be Vera. And eventually she did.

Vera went to New York and talked to every employee who had been with the studio in Florida. Most of them were studio old-timers, good friends of Vera's, and deeply loyal to Max. No one knew anything about the missing papers.

The one person Vera hadn't spoken to was Charlie, the mechanical genius, and the only Fleischer brother to remain in Florida with his family. She phoned Charlie, who said he didn't know anything about missing papers. However, he said, his son, Ozzie, had worked at the Miami studio as a sort of handyman. Maybe he knew something. Indeed, he did. He knew all about it.

What Ozzie had to say confirmed Max's worst fears. The papers had been burned. This was not a hearsay report. Ozzie was an eyewitness and a participant. He told of porters carting load after load of papers of every description, including books, most of them marked *Fleischer Studios,* and dumping them near an open fire. Other porters threw the records into the flames.

The Paramount representative in charge of this operation was Dick Murray, the same Dick Murray who handed Max the disastrous, unilateral contract that killed Fleischer Studios. Now he watched over its cremation. He watched as twelve years of corporate records, statements, tax reports, production records, film delivery records, and laboratory, payroll, and social security records for over seven hundred employees turned into a pile of ashes. It took two or three days to burn out the history of Fleischer Studios. But it didn't burn out the tormenting question that was eating away at Max's insides, the question that he had put to Balaban in New York: "What is the purpose of all this?"

The Jam Handy Organization specialized in producing educational-industrial motion pictures as well as slide films. Max felt strongly that all educational as well as all training films should be entertaining in order to keep their audiences interested. He soon became aware that the writing staff at this company didn't have a clue about how to do this.

He immediately wrote a thirty-four-page "bible" applying the theory and practice of motion picture script techniques to the presentation of industrial and educational films. The scriptwriters lapped it up like parched wolves. Their screenplays took on a new and improved look.

Over the next few years, Max turned his remarkably inventive mind to various elements with which the Handy Organization dealt. The result was a whole series of patents that, by contract, Max shared with the company. Here are just a few of many:

Synchronized Slidefilm Projector
A New Use for Electric Conductive Ink
Copy Reader: A Means of Assisting Galley-Proof
    Readers
A Method for Using Paper Film for Projection Instead
    of Reflection
Record Timing Device

A Means of Evaluating Audience Reactions to Motion Picture, Radio, or Stage Presentation

The "Synchronized Slidefilm Projector" was meant to address the problem that, up to the time of this invention, it was very difficult to get sound, which was on a moving track, synchronized with the slide film, which was on a stationary disk. The "Means of Evaluating Audience Reactions" predated the now-famous Gallup Poll and is basically still in use today.

Inventing, by itself, wasn't enough to satisfy an artistically creative psyche. In 1944, Max took on the job of producing and directing one of the Handy Organization's rare theatrical animated cartoons. Not surprisingly, the picture turned out to be a classic, one that was tremendously popular worldwide then and remains so today: *Rudolph the Red Nosed Reindeer.*

22

It seems that Max's aim in life was to be fully occupied and challenged all the time. He had an enormous capacity for creative work. However, his mind reached out in so many different directions that I don't believe he could ever be completely satisfied. In fact, in the middle of all the inventing and film producing that he was doing for the Handy Organization, he was getting restless. I find the following note from Max to Jam Handy revealing and touching. It is a mental giant's cry for help:

> Dear Jam:
>
> My full knowledge and ability to assist JHO in many directions has never been utilized. Will the future offer such an opportunity?

Apparently, Max felt that it wouldn't. A few years later, he was back in New York, living at the Windermere Hotel, in apartment 11J, the same apartment in which he and Essie had always lived.

Max spent the next few years commuting between New York and Detroit, supervising the Jam Handy productions and the development of his many inventions, like one of the most important and widely used inventions ever created for motion pictures, Rear Screen Projection, as well as 3-D movies that didn't require special glasses. He lectured at various schools and universities; wrote a delightful book, *Noah's Shoes,* published in 1951; put together a mail-order animation course that included a thirteen-page manual and a miniature animation table; and kept a careful watch on that burgeoning new entertainment upstart, television.

During this period, a strange and rather odd thing happened. In 1953, Max resigned from the Jam Handy Organization and signed a contract with Bray Studios, the same studio for which he had worked in New York in 1916 at the very beginning of his career, the same J. R. Bray with whom he had worked at the *Brooklyn Daily Eagle* in 1902. How this arrangement came about, I have no idea. Did Max seek Bray out, or was it the other way around? Would going back to Bray look like Max's career was in reverse?

My excuse for not being fully aware of the Bray connection was that I was pursuing my career in Hollywood and was, literally, totally immersed in directing *Twenty Thousand Leagues under the Sea* for, of all people, Walt Disney.

In any event, on March 2, 1953, Max and Bray Studios signed an agreement setting up the Bray-Fleischer Division of Bray Studios, Inc. The two pioneers in the field of animated cartoons and technical drawings would concentrate on, among other things, new techniques in 3-D film cartoons for the theatrical and industrial fields. The Bray-Fleischer relationship lasted until at least 1956, but unfortunately, I can find no record of what, if anything, was ever created.

Max watched as a new medium, television, grew into a ravening beast, stuffing itself with every form of entertainment known to the public. He watched and wondered what would happen to the hundreds of his cartoons in Paramount's possession. He finally found out when, in 1955, Paramount announced the sale of all its shorts, some two thousand of them, to various television outlets, including those owned by Paramount, for $4.5 million dollars. Naturally, all 661 of the Fleischer product were included.

The sale of all the Paramount shorts to television wasn't at all surprising. What was surprising was that it hadn't taken place sooner. After all, Paramount was the first motion picture company to recognize the importance of television, having formed, in 1939, Paramount Television Productions, Inc., which operated Station KTLA in Hollywood. Max's question to Balaban, "What is the purpose of all this?" was suddenly, in Max's mind, answered.

The Fleischer Studios agreements with King Features, beginning in 1932, in which the studio obtained motion picture rights to Popeye and other characters associated with the *Thimble Theatre* comic strip, required Fleischer to destroy each *Popeye* cartoon, and all its elements, as it reached ten years in distribution. To make certain that this destruction, which was to begin in November 1942, actually took place, the contract required that Fleischer Studios furnish affidavits that the *Popeyes* were, indeed, destroyed.

When the first contract was drawn with King Features in 1932, there were very few television sets in the entire country.

And then, too, no one could possibly conceive, let alone antici-
pate, the howling success of the *Popeye* cartoons. Certainly, by
the time 1941 rolled around, both Paramount and King Features saw the folly of destroying those cartoons.

Max must have reasoned that King Features would have
welcomed a suggestion from Paramount that the agreement be
revised so that the *Popeyes* would be saved. He must have further reasoned that Paramount would rather split the proceeds
from this tremendously successful series two ways rather than
three. Of course, the only way to do that would be to destroy
Fleischer Studios. With Fleischer Studios out of the picture,
Paramount could assure King Features that splitting the profits
fifty-fifty was perfectly legal.

These were all surmises on Max's part. He didn't have as
much as a piece of paper to back him up. Somehow, all his
papers had disappeared.

It wasn't too long before the *Popeye* and *Betty Boop* cartoons
began showing up on television screens in homes all over the
country. Max couldn't believe what he was looking at. Not only
had the name Fleischer Studios been replaced by the name Famous Studios, but most galling of all, his own credit, "PRODUCED
BY MAX FLEISCHER," had been completely deleted. Some of the
cartoons had the audacity to credit the head of Paramount Pictures, Adolf Zukor, as producer.

Max also watched with horrified eyes the brutal reediting
of some of the cartoons, particularly the two-reelers that didn't
fit into a normal television time slot. In one of his many memos,
he describes a particularly destructive example: "The major por-
tion of our two-reel color cartoon titled, 'Ali Baba' was used to
create a cartoon titled, 'Popeye Makes A Movie,' by slicing up

our picture, and adding a few scenes made by Famous Studios, in order to bring it down to a one-reeler. About 80% of our picture was used, my credit deleted and in its place, 'Famous Studios' applied their credit. . . . In all my experience in the industry, I have never seen, or heard of a more dastardly man-handling of the works of producers." This was, obviously, a deeply angry, painfully wounded man.

I was becoming more and more concerned about my father's health. He had suffered from ulcers for many years, but now, with what was happening to his films, his condition worsened. He was becoming more and more reclusive.

The year 1955 was coming to an end, and it reminded me that Christmas Eve would be my parents' fiftieth wedding an-niversary. I felt that a change of scenery would do my father good, get his mind off the aggravating things that were happen-ing to him. So, with a lot of urging from my sister, Ruth, as well as from my mother, Essie, we prevailed on him to spend his golden wedding anniversary with me and my wife, Mickey, and our three wonderful kids, Bruce, Mark, and Jane, in California.

It turned out to be a good idea. My mother had made fairly frequent visits to us on the Coast, but my father never had. In fact, this was only his second trip to California. The first one had been many years earlier, when I was about fifteen years old. He had taken my mother and me to a Paramount convention that was held at the Ambassador Hotel in Los Angeles.

On this trip, he was free of all obligations and seemed to find real enjoyment being with our kids. The kids were abso-lutely crazy about "Popa Max." And then there was an addi-tional, unexpected event that made this trip truly memorable and, in a way, historic.

I gave the news of my father's visit to the top gossip columnist in Hollywood, Army Archerd, whose daily column appeared in the famous trade paper *Variety*. Archerd's column was, and still is, the first thing everyone reads in the paper. The following day, I got a call from Walt Disney. "I see your father's in town," he said. "I think we should meet. Why don't you bring him over to the studio? I'll round up some of his boys, and we'll have lunch." I was touched by this gesture, and so was my father.

Max had never met Walt, but I certainly had. My relationship with him was extraordinary, almost beyond belief. I couldn't help thinking back on my own first meeting with Walt. It was a meeting that changed my life and my career.

My meeting with Walt Disney happened a few years earlier, in 1952, when I was still considered a young, relatively inexperienced Hollywood director of low-budget movies. But I was on the rise, with a very good small picture to my credit, *The Narrow Margin*, that had garnered high critical praise. I followed that with a larger-budgeted film, *The Happy Time*, that was also well received. Still, I was a long way from where I wanted to be. I was still dreaming of directing big-budget films with big stars and long shooting schedules. Then "the Disney miracle" happened.

I was at home worrying about where my next movie was coming from when I was contacted by my agent, Ray Stark. He told me he'd just received a strange phone call from Walt Disney.

"Yeah? What did he want?" I asked.

"He wants to see you," came the reply.

"*Me?* He wants to see *me?*" I was incredulous. "You've got to be kidding."

"No, he wants to see you at ten tomorrow morning at his office. Can you be there?"

I was perplexed. "Well, what does he want to see me about?"

"He didn't say, just that he'd like you to come to his office. How about it?"

"Well, I guess so," I replied, a bit tentatively. "I'll be there. Are you sure he wants to see *me?*"

"That's what he said."

I was uncomfortable driving onto the Disney lot in Burbank. This was enemy territory—Mickey Mouse Lane, Donald Duck Walk. I finally found my way to Walt's office. There he was, standing behind his desk, smiling warmly: my father's nemesis. We shook hands. A Fleischer shaking hands with a Disney? I felt that it was a minor historic moment, but I didn't mention it, and neither did he. Card Walker and Bill Walsh, two of the company's top executives, were also there, and Disney introduced me to them.

I sat and waited expectantly for Disney to get to the point of this exercise. I didn't have to wait long. He pointed to the wall opposite his desk. "You familiar with that story?" he asked.

I looked where he indicated. On the wall, obviously temporarily tacked up, was a large watercolor painting, vividly rendered in dramatic colors, of a strange-looking craft entangled in the tentacles of a giant squid. Below it was the legend, in baroque lettering, *Twenty Thousand Leagues under the Sea.*

"Of course," I said. "Who isn't familiar with it? I don't think there's anyone who hasn't read that book."

"That's right," he agreed. "That's why we're going to make a movie of it."

"Sounds terrific. Animated, of course."

"No, this'll be an all-live-action feature. And it'll be, by far, the most expensive picture we've ever made, about three and a half million." I gave a low whistle. In the early 1950s, that was as big as they came. "We're negotiating for James Mason to play Captain Nemo and Kirk Douglas for Ned Land," he continued, mentioning two of the biggest screen stars of the day.

"They should be great." I was genuinely impressed.

"And we want you to direct it."

"Me?" I wasn't sure I'd heard right.

Walt nodded and smiled broadly at my reaction. I shook my head in disbelief. The big picture with big stars, the thing I'd dreamed of, was being dropped in my lap by, of all people, Walt Disney.

"I'm overwhelmed," I said. "Certainly I want to direct it. But why me? Why do you want me to do it?"

A big grin covered his face. "We saw your picture *The Happy Time*." I remembered then that young Bobby Driscoll, who'd played the lead in it, also starred in Disney's *Song of the South*. "Well," Walt continued, "anybody who can make an actor out of Bobby Driscoll has got to be a great director."

All of us burst into laughter. Walt got up from his desk and walked over to me. "How about it? Are you coming to work for us?"

I got up too and studied him and the others in the room for a moment, trying to get a clue from their faces. Then I said, "You do know who I am, don't you?"

Walt chuckled. "Yes, we know. That doesn't make any difference."

"That's wonderful because more than anything in the world I want to do this picture. But I can't accept it without talking it over with my father first. I'm afraid he might think I'm disloyal or something. If he did, I just couldn't do it."

"I understand," Walt said, as he walked me to the door of his office. "You're absolutely right. You talk to your father tonight and call me tomorrow morning."

I phoned my father in New York as soon as I got home, told him the whole story, and held my breath. "Of course you should do that picture," he reassured me. "You didn't have to call me. You go right ahead and take the job."

"You sure?"

"Absolutely. And you tell Walt one thing from me."

"What's that?"

"You tell Walt that I said he's got great taste in directors."

The story of that meeting got around. Even now, when I'm introduced to people, they frequently ask: "Are you the director who had to ask his father's permission to make a movie?"

On January 4, 1956, the two great animators met. This time, the Fleischer/Disney handshake was truly important. Walt was a charming, flattering host. My father seemed to be enjoying himself, but, in Walt's presence, he seemed diminished, and my heart broke for him. I had the feeling that Goliath had defeated David.

We took a tour of the studio and had lunch in the commissary. Many of my father's ex-employees, "his boys," showed up, and there were plenty of in-jokes and fond reminiscences. There is a historic picture of the event with everyone's signature on it. On the bottom of the picture is a large, hand-drawn scroll bearing the legend: "Inkwell Reunion, or What Cartoons Can Do to Cartoonists. Jan. 4 1956."

23

Leonard Miltonberg ran a company in Manhattan called Inventors Intermediaries. Inventors would come to him if they had something that they thought was marketable, and he would try to find an outlet for their work. Early in 1956, Max paid a visit to Miltonberg's office. He had with him a new type of slide projector on which he held the patent. Instead of the conventional flat glass slides, this device used a small disc rimmed with tiny pictures. When projected, one at a time, the tiny pictures told a story, in this case *Rudolph the Red Nosed Reindeer.* A disc containing pictures for projection certainly sounds like the forerunner of DVD technology.

Miltonberg was not alone in his office. He had with him a young lawyer fresh out of Harvard Law School by the name of Stanley Handman. Handman had completed his business with Miltonberg, but when he learned that Max Fleischer was on the way in, he stayed to meet this man whose work he greatly admired.

Talk about the right man, in the right place, at the right time. This meeting with Handman went way beyond such an everyday, mundane coincidence. Handman was heaven-sent. He was a knight in shining armor. He was a miracle worker.

Handman, like everyone else in the industry, knew about the Paramount/Fleischer blowup and, like everyone else, was curious about what had happened. He stuck around and asked Max out for coffee at the deli across the street.

It didn't take much encouragement to get Max started about the Paramount situation. Handman was fascinated. There was no way an interested, inquisitive listener could get anywhere near the whole story over a cup of coffee. From Handman's questions, Max felt that he was getting a sympathetic ear and invited Handman to the Windermere apartment for lunch the following day if he wished to hear more. He did, and the long, sordid story continued well past lunch the next day.

When Max got to the end of the story, the selling of all the Paramount shorts to television outlets, and voiced his utter frustration at not being able to do a damn thing without any documents to back him up, Handman reluctantly had to agree. The whole thing looked hopeless. An action against Paramount just wasn't possible.

As an afterthought, Max mentioned his anger and frustration at the massacre of his films, the reediting and brutalization of his work, the replacement of the Fleischer Studios screen credit, and, finally, the total elimination of his name from all his films. Handman sat bolt upright in his chair and almost shouted two words, two magic words, that changed the whole complexion of what they'd been discussing: "That's actionable!"

The words hit Max's ears like an exploding bomb. Finally,

he had a case against Paramount. He could raise his voice in a court of law and be heard.

Why he waited so long before he took any legal action at all has always been a matter of speculation in the industry. Was it because he could see no way around the fact that, on his attorney's advice, he signed the disastrous 1941 contract? Did the mysterious disappearance of all his records and papers make him believe that a case against Paramount was hopeless? Or was it his deep concern for the welfare of his daughter, Ruth, and her husband, Seymour, and their family?

Whatever the reason, after fifteen years of waiting, of refusing to take legal action of any kind against his tormentor, of silently and painfully eating himself alive, he suddenly made up his mind. It was time to step into the arena. It was time to fight back.

Like any other legal action, this one could not proceed until papers, documents, proofs, had been produced. But the situation now was very different than the situation had been fifteen years earlier. The evidence that Max and Handman needed was right there in front of them. In fact, it was right there in front of anyone who cared to look at a television screen. All that needed to be done was to document it.

Max and his devoted secretary, Vera Coleman, set up a sort of screening room in the living room of the Windermere apartment. They had two television sets, and sometimes three, that were turned on all day long and well into the night, each tuned to a different channel, each searching out a Fleischer cartoon. They would jot down the date and exact time of the showing of the picture, the title, the distributor, the producer's credit, and any editing changes and deletions as well as the names of all advertised products.

At the end of each session, Vera would type all the notes that she and Max had made. It was a fatiguing, eye-straining job, but they kept at it week after week, month after month, filling up innumerable notebooks. The apartment was beginning to look like an annex to the Library of Congress. And still they went on and on. The more evidence they could present to a court, the stronger their case would become, and the greater the amount of damages that could be claimed.

On April 2, 1956, Max reestablished Fleischer Studios, Inc., in New York, and on June 17, 1956, Handman took action against Paramount, Warner Brothers, National Telefilm Associates, DuMont Broadcasting, and all others involved in the sale of the Fleischer product to television outlets. The action, filed in the New York State Supreme Court, asked for $2,750,000 for the films being televised "without proper credit and authority." It also sought an injunction permanently restraining the television broadcasting of any of the Fleischer movies.

The case involved Max's claim that his product could not be legally presented on television in connection with commercial advertising. It also involved the claim that the credits had been "altered and mutilated" with the result that his reputation had been damaged. This second half of the complaint stood on somewhat rocky ground since it was based on Article 6 of the Berne Treaty, which reads: "Independently of the author's economic rights, and even after the transfer of said rights, the author shall have the right to claim authorship of the work and to object to any distortion, mutilation or other modification of, or other derogatory action in relation to, the said work, which would be prejudicial to his honor or reputation."

Article 6 of the Berne Treaty fit Max's complaint like melted wax poured into a mold. The only problem was that, while every other civilized country in the world had signed the treaty, the United States had not. Still, Max and Handman felt that it was worth making reference to the treaty during a trial because its weighty prestige in the Western world might have some influence in an American court of law. (The United States joined the Berne Treaty in 1989.)

Besides his deeply held conviction about the righteousness of his case, Max also harbored an underlying hope that something else might happen. During the preparation of any legal case, pretrial discovery must be made. That is, all individuals connected with the action, whether important or minor, are subpoenaed to testify under oath about what they know concerning the matter at hand. Pretrial discovery would obviously be a golden opportunity to put Paramount executives on the stand and demand documents. They would then have to testify under oath about what had really happened to Fleischer Studios. And they might, they just might, reveal the location of the smoking gun, the evidence that would void the 1941 contract that had destroyed Fleischer Studios, deprived Max of all his copyrights, patents, and inventions, and, indeed, destroyed his life.

On June 19, a few days after the case was filed, Max held a press conference in New York. The following day, the story was headline news. Of course, given the connection with cartoons, the press couldn't resist having a little fun. "POPEYE'S PAPA SUES PARAMOUNT," ran the headline in the *New York Journal American*. *Variety* gave the story the front page and the headline "MAX FLEISCHER FILES $2,750,000 SUIT TO NEGATE PAR'S SALE OF HIS OLD SHORTS TO TV."

All the newspaper coverage carried a statement that Max

had made at the close of the press conference. To me, his son, it is the most moving statement I've ever read. It contains so much insight about his pain, his anger, his deep hurt, and most of all his wounded dignity. It says:

> It is my intention to prevent the improper exploitation of my reputation and the films which I produced. In certain instances credits have been inserted which mislead the public by giving credit to people who never had anything to do with the production of my films. I will not consent to being relegated to anonymity by allowing others to reap the artistic prominence and financial reward of my lifetime of creative work in the motion picture field.

24

Max was kept busy. He wrote myriad and lengthy memos, trying to remember as many details of past events as he could. With Handman he arranged, prepared for, and attended the depositions of the many parties involved in the case. Both he and Handman worked long, long hours. And still no smoking gun surfaced.

It wasn't until October 14, 1957, that Dave took the plunge and brought his own suit against Paramount. Up to this time he was in court fighting a case against him for nonsupport of his family. In his Paramount case, however, he did a curious thing: he named Max as a defendant. How he intended to prove that Max aided and abetted Paramount in destroying his own studios was a matter of bemused curiosity.

Oddly enough, Dave's case began to look as though it might be quite helpful to Max's suit, particularly when it came to the pretrial depositions. Some of the earliest witnesses called to testify in Dave's action were two of the most important for Max's case, Dick Murray and Lou Phillips. If these Paramount executives could be put in the position of having to explain why they created the unilateral 1941 contract, the goal of negating that contract might actually be accomplished.

It fell to Dick Murray, Paramount's official contact with Fleischer Studios, to supply the following information about the studio's destruction: "During the course of production of 'Gulliver's Travels,' a great—and disruptive—personal conflict arose between Dave Fleischer and his brother Max. Their personal animosity grew to such an extent that they were not even on speaking terms with each other. This feud between the brothers was a matter of general knowledge in the Studios. Morale suffered and any effective operation of the Studios was rendered impossible."

In his deposition, Lou Phillips, a Paramount lawyer and vice president, similarly tried to put forward a logical and believable explanation: "By 1941," he said, "it had become apparent that the Fleischer Studios operation was unsuccessful and in financial straits. Very heavy advances by Paramount were unrecouped. Max and Dave were at loggerheads, and their feud was disrupting their operations. The Fleischer Studios difficulties were further complicated by the fact that the Studios had been moved from New York to Florida."

Forewarned is forearmed. With that testimony in hand, Max could prepare himself to answer the accusations.

That the brothers were feuding there is no question. According to Max, the accusation that their enmity had an effect on the efficiency with which the studio was run was patently untrue. The studio kept to its production schedules without a snag. There were no delays or postponements in the release of any production—and this in the midst of the monumental move from New York to Miami, the regular production of cartoons and other shorts, and the preparation of *Gulliver' Travels*, the studio's first feature-length cartoon. Especially given that *Gulliver* was completed within eighteen months of Paramount approving the script—not to mention two months early—it's more than a little difficult to credit assertions that Max and Dave's feuding was disrupting studio operations. One wonders too just how concerned Paramount could have been when, immediately on the very successful release of *Gulliver,* it ordered a second feature, *Mr. Bug Goes to Town,* as well as twelve *Popeyes,* twelve *Superman* shorts, and a raft of two-reel and standard cartoons.

And then there are the charges put forth by Phillips that the studio was deeply in debt to Paramount. That is perfectly true.

When Paramount decided to go ahead with the making of *Gulliver* and the building of a new animation studio in Miami, it was clear that considerable amounts of money were going to be spent. Since Paramount and Fleischer were still working under an early contract, it was obvious that a new contract had to be created for this present situation in 1938.

As Max points out in one of his documents, in this new 1938 contract Paramount clearly states that all expenses incurred by Fleischer Studios in moving from New York to Miami, plus the cost of building a new studio, would be amortized over a period of ten years. Max goes on to explain: "Throughout the 1938 contract it is evident that money was advanced to the Fleischer Studios for two purposes. Advances were made strictly for the purpose of production and for no other use. Such sums did not increase the Studios' indebtedness in any manner. If

Paramount was unable to recoup such sums, the Studios were in no way responsible."

Also according to Max: "Loans were made to the Studios for the purchase of real estate, building construction, and other matters which had no bearing on production." These loans came to about a half million dollars. Concerning this money Max writes: "From my viewpoint, after careful study of the entire operation, I believe that Paramount could have, if they so desired, arranged for the Studios to receive sufficient royalties to liquidate all the loans in less than ten years."

What happened was that Paramount did indeed loan Fleischer Studios a lot of money, contractually allowing ten years for it to be paid back. Then, out of the blue, in May 1941, after three years of working under the 1938 contract, Fleischer Studios was sent a new contract canceling all previous contracts, agreements, and obligations to finance or pay any money and demanding that all assets be turned over to Paramount. It was a contract that no one at Fleischer Studios had ever heard of before, much less negotiated, and furthermore one that Max and Dave were given a few days at most to consider, under threat of a payroll cutoff.

So, take your pick. Which version do you choose?

25

The lawsuit against Paramount et al., the possibility of somehow negating the ruinous 1941 contract, the chance of telling how he had signed the contract under duress, all this was something of a tonic for Max. It seemed that the tide was turning. It even seemed that the tide might be turning into something of a wave.

A longtime friend and admirer of Max's, a chap named Hal Seeger, approached Max with an interesting proposition. Seeger was the president of Hal Seeger Productions, a New York animation company that serviced big advertising agencies such as BBD&O and many other distinguished corporations like RCA, Campbell Soups, General Electric, and Westinghouse. In other words, he was a genuine producer and could be taken seriously.

What Seeger wanted to do was revive and produce for television Ko-Ko the Clown and the *Out of the Inkwell* cartoon series as well as the bouncing ball *Screen Songs,* all of which

Max had originated forty years earlier. Seeger had it all thought out. He and Max would be equal partners. Seeger would be the producer; Max would act as a consultant. They would make one hundred five-minute color cartoons. Each cartoon would open with Max in live action at the animation board, drawing and bringing Ko-Ko to life, just like the good old days. Max would also bring his vast expertise to the project as well as his many new concepts of how to drastically cut animation costs.

Not only had Seeger thought it all out, but he had even gone so far as to contact some financiers, the Berger brothers, who ran a company known as Video House. The Bergers were gung ho about the project.

Max's feelings must have been a mixture of joy, pride, and bittersweet emotions as he absorbed all this. How did he feel about the title *consultant* instead of *studio head?* And did he realize that, as encouraging as all this was, his life was still in a reverse cycle? Ko-Ko the Clown was, after all, the first cartoon he had created at the very beginning of his career.

But that was not the last stop in the reverse cycle. When the time came to start photography of Max at the drawing board, he wanted to look younger. He decided to dye his white hair dark brown. My mother, Essie, took the first stab at the dye job. Max's hair turned out green. He let a professional take over. What he was doing, in fact, was going backward in time, toward his youth.

Some pills are harder to swallow, more bitter than others, but as far as his outward demeanor was concerned, Max was excited; he was professionally and happily occupied in the field in which he excelled. He was the same sweet, funny, gentle, caring guy we always knew and always loved.

Out of the Inkwell, Inc., was reestablished on January 14, 1958, with production of the series starting on February 10. Ko-Ko the Clown was redesigned to give him a more modern look, and a girlfriend, Kokette, was supplied for him. Other new characters such as KoKonut and Mean Moe also joined the cartoon cast. The year 1958 ended on a very positive note.

In a surprisingly short period of time, Out of the Inkwell was producing five-minute color cartoons at the rate of one a week. Eventually, one hundred were actually made. And the cartoons were moderately successful, although no blockbusters these. Video House sold its ownership to another distributing company, and ownership of the cartoons started to pass from hand to hand as other companies bought them and took a crack at trying to make a go of them.

Things looked most promising when Seven Arts bought the distribution rights and came out, on October 23, 1963, with a full-page ad in *Variety* announcing its acquisition. But Seven Arts had no better luck than the others in trying to get the Ko-Ko cartoons off the ground and onto television screens. Then, on December 3, 1964, *Variety* announced the dissolution of Out of the Inkwell, Inc.

Once again Cervantes was right. Ill luck seldom comes alone. And along came more. After more than five years of being an action pending in the courts, the suit against Paramount et al. was suddenly no longer pending. It was over. Paramount had entered a summary judgment plea that Max's case be thrown out of court. It was granted. Too much time had elapsed before bringing the case to court. The statute of limitations had run its course.

It was over. Finished. The case was never heard on its merits.

The decision was not unexpected by any means since Dave's case had been decided against him for the same reason about a year before. Still, there had been hope that, before the court calendar caught up with Max and Handman, the pretrial investigations, the sworn depositions, even a slip of the tongue, would yield something useful. But nothing did.

There is a saying that, if it weren't for hope, the heart would break. Well, the summary judgment took away all hope, and my father's heart broke. And not just his heart broke, but his spirit, his health, and, eventually, his mind broke as well.

The loss of the case was not, however, a total defeat. Some good actually came from it. During the years of litigation, many of the companies being sued restored Max's credit to its proper place in their films. But this one small victory was Pyrrhic at best.

I was in Los Angeles when my sister, Ruth, phoned me from New York with the news about the summary judgment. A tremendous wave of sadness covered me. "This will kill him," I said. "No," she answered. "You don't know Pops. He'll find something, some angle, some new approach. He'll never let go."

I knew that my father would need moral support, and since he truly loved my wife, Mickey, and our three young children, we took off for New York to see if we could bring some modicum of cheer into his life. And I really believe we did. He adored the kids, and they worshiped their Popa Max. But I soon found out from Ruth and her wonderful husband, Seymour, the most shocking, the most unbelievable news I'd ever heard in my life: my folks, my mother and father, were broke, virtually penniless. They were living mostly on their social security checks.

26

The whole thing was incomprehensible to me. My folks broke? How was that possible? Money was never an issue in our family. Anything I wanted I got, without question or hesitation. When I graduated from public school and wanted to go to an expensive prep school, Peekskill Military Academy, because a friend of mine went there—and, besides, I liked the uniform—I went to Peekskill. In fact, when the academy got hard up for cash, my father bailed it out of the hole. When I wanted to go to Brown University and then to the Yale School of Drama, both pricey universities, I went. When I said I needed a car, my parents got me a Packard convertible.

And what about my folks, with their chauffeur-driven, twelve-cylinder Packard limousine? What about the estate in Miami Beach? Weren't they still residing in apartment 11J at the elegant Windermere Hotel? There were no indications I could see that things had gotten this bad—or even bad at all.

It had been at least twenty years since my father had lost the original Fleischer Studios. During that time, his income from the Jam Handy Organization and from J. R. Bray was modest. The Miami Beach estate was long gone, sold well below its market value. The limo and its driver bit the dust as well.

Surely, one would think, Max would have accumulated a very sizable retirement fund from royalties generated by the tremendously successful *Screen Songs, Betty Boop, Popeye the Sailor,* and *Superman* cartoons. It's true that lawsuits suck up money with the same zest that anteaters suck up ants, and the Paramount case had been no exception. It certainly did its job. It took five years of litigation to reduce whatever funds Max had to almost nothing. His faithful and devoted secretary, Vera Coleman, survived on a minuscule salary and social security while she typed the voluminous memos and legal documents.

Stanley Handman, as Max's representative, had done his best to keep expenses down. In fact, he went well beyond the call of duty. He trimmed his fees as things got tighter until he was working pro bono. He stayed with the case to the very end, even beyond the end.

As soon as I learned of the financial situation, I insisted that I help my parents and Vera. I certainly wasn't one of Hollywood's highest-paid directors, but I knew I had to do something. Ruth and Seymour had done all that they could afford, but it wasn't easy for them to do much since their lives had been disrupted by a terrible tragedy: their two young sons had contracted polio simultaneously (these were the pre–Salk vaccine days) and were hospitalized for more than a year. The emotional and financial distress was almost beyond belief.

In any event, in spite of strong protests from my father, I

worked out a monthly budget for my parents and Vera. They could now stop worrying about the rent, food, utilities, and other expenses. It wasn't lavish, but it was enough.

My father smiled for the first time since we arrived in New York. For me, it was emotionally devastating. It was simply unthinkable that he should be in such financial straits. How could such a thing happen? It wasn't until I started to write this book and began going through my father's papers and documents that I began to get some idea.

The first cartoons that Max produced for Paramount, in 1929, were the sing-along bouncing ball *Screen Songs*. They were quick, easy, and very inexpensive to make. And they were hugely successful. Paramount was taken completely by surprise. How much of a surprise, and how much of an embarrassment to some executives, is apparent from the following letter, dated July 9, 1957, that Max sent to Stanley Handman:

Dear Stanley,

To the best of my recollections, I attended a Paramount convention in California about 1932 or 1933.

At that time, Emanuel Cohen was vice-president of Paramount (or Famous Artists Lasky).

He called me aside in one of the meeting rooms at the Convention hotel (The Ambassador, I believe) and told me that he and the high-ups in Paramount were very much surprised at the way the "Screen Songs" were selling. He said they had no idea they would be such a tremendous success.

This situation, Cohen said, reflected upon him, because my contract would mean a great deal of money to me (Fleischer Studios) but would mean very little to Paramount. In Cohen's words: "They're all shouting about the Screen Songs, and you, Max, will be about the only one to benefit." Then he said, "Max, you can say 'NO' to my request, if you like, to revise our contract in order that Paramount get a fairer share of the deal." He further explained that, in the belief that the idea of "Screen Songs" would be just "so-so" he slanted the deal in my favor, but they turned out to be a Movie Hit.

Naturally, I said that I did not like to feel we had a one-sided contract. . . .

So naturally, or perhaps unnaturally, Max allowed the contract to be revised.

Can you imagine this situation being reversed? Paramount thinks Max made a bad deal for himself, so they offer to reduce their profit and give him more money? Max's reaction to Cohen's proposal, however, reveals a true insight into his character: he was a man of high moral principle, of fairness, of ethics.

With the addition of the *Betty Boop* series and, shortly after that, the *Popeye* series, Fleischer Studios was on a roll. Even with the new, rewritten contract, the financial rewards were becoming evident. As Max states in another of his pretrial memos: "Quarterly checks due . . . were handed to me by Lou Diamond or Dick Murray. As near as I can recall, the royalty figures climbed steadily until they reached the sum of (for one quarter) $14,000.00. I do not remember who handed me this top figure check, but I believe it was Dick Murray. In handing me the check, the following remark was made: 'The top Paramount Boys say that you're making too much money.'"

Although the cartoons had lost none of their steam at the box office, the next quarter's royalty came in at around $9,000. Quarter by quarter, the royalty checks kept dropping until, two years later, they stopped altogether.

When Max made inquiries into what was happening, he was told that the cartoons were getting harder and harder to sell, that, in fact, Paramount was in the red as far as the cartoons were concerned. But still they kept releasing them.

Max asked if Paramount had any idea of discontinuing the cartoons. The answer he got was: "No, the exhibitors want them, but they don't pay much for them. The situation may change, but, just now, that's it." In spite of the continued popularity and high ratings of the cartoons for the next ten years, Max contends that not a single dollar in royalty was ever paid again.

The most puzzling aspect of this whole business of no royalties for what appeared to be hugely successful cartoons was Max's attitude. It was one of laissez-faire, strictly hands-off. Surely he must have been aware that something funny was going on. Only it wasn't so funny. One of the broadest suggestions that something was amiss came from William Brandt, a good friend of Max's. Brandt owned and ran a chain of fifty theaters, loved the Fleischer cartoons, and wanted them for his theaters but couldn't get them. One day he phoned Max complaining about this situation. Brandt told him that, even after he offered Paramount more than the other chains paid, he was still turned down.

Max asked his Paramount contact, Lou Diamond, to investigate. According to Max, Diamond came up with this: "You better keep your nose out of distribution and tend to your productions if you don't want a bellyful of trouble."

If anything ever screamed out for an audit, this was it. But, no, Max did nothing. The only reason that I can think of for not auditing was that he was afraid of offending the Paramount executives. An audit, he must have figured, would surely be taken to mean that he didn't trust them, that he was casting aspersions on their integrity and honesty. My father was too much of a gentleman to do that.

Even more inexplicable was Max's reaction to an offer made by Emanuel Cohen, by that time a former vice president of Paramount. Perhaps his mishandling of the bouncing ball *Screen Songs* had something to do with his new title of former vice president. In any event, the following incident is memorialized by Max in a pretrial memo:

> Shortly after Vice-President, Emanuel Cohen, was dismissed from Paramount Cohen invited me to his home and made me the following offer:
>
> He intended going into business for himself and asked me to refuse renewal of contract with Paramount and join him. I refused, saying that I believed we would eventually make money, even though it seemed difficult at the time. Mr. Cohen offered to deposit a half million dollars in any bank of my choice, the money to be used for production. He wanted no stock. All he wanted was distribution of the product. He said he wanted no red tape to hinder me. Accordingly, the entire deposit would be subject to withdrawal for production on my signature alone. I did wonder why a product which apparently lost money for Paramount seemed to be so attractive to Emanuel Cohen.
>
> I turned Cohen's proposal down with: "Sorry Mannie,

but my lot is cast with Paramount. I still believe I'll come out all right." Mannie said, "If you don't know how Paramount is doing you, you'll find out when it's too late."

Max ended the memo with these words: "He was right."

If what Max recorded in this memo is true, then it gives the lie to Paramount's insistence that the cartoons weren't making any profit. Mannie Cohen had unquestionably been in a position to know how the cartoons were doing. The sweetheart deal he offered Max speaks for itself. If the cartoons weren't making big profits, he would have been crazy to make such an offer.

On the other hand, you'd have to be crazy to turn down such an offer. I can only conjecture as to why Max walked away from the deal. Was it that his sense of honor and loyalty wouldn't permit it? He'd signed a contract with Paramount; he'd given his word to play by the rules; he'd cast his lot with them. He couldn't accept the idea that they would not play fair with him. In spite of all signs to the contrary, in spite of all the red flags waving, he still believed that he'd come out all right. And that's why he ended up broke.

27

Our family was not one that regularly read the business pages of the newspapers, so we all missed an article that would change our lives forever. But Stanley Handman read the *Wall Street Journal,* and he didn't miss it. Thank God.

The article concerned a new copyright law that Congress had just passed. The old copyright law stated that, if the original author had assigned his rights to a third party (which Paramount did when it sold all the Fleischer cartoons), the copyright would run for twenty-eight years and could be renewed for an additional twenty-eight years. After the second twenty-eight years had expired, the author's work became public domain and could be used by anyone without either payment or permission of the author.

This, of course, was old stuff to Stanley. It was what came next that was a real grabber, a jaw dropper, an eye popper. The new law stated that, if the author hadn't assigned renewal rights (which Max never did) and was still alive (which Max certainly was), only he had the right to renew.

Stanley picked himself up off the floor and read the article two or three more times to make sure that it said what it seemed to say. It did. No third party could renew the almost-expired *Betty Boop* copyright, whatever rights the party claimed to have. Only the living author, Max, could do that.

Stanley raced to the Windermere and gave the news to Max, Essie, and Vera. I can imagine the scene when Stanley read the newspaper article to them. I can imagine it, but not having been there, I can't describe it. Who could? Who can describe the indescribable?

In timely fashion, Stanley had Max sign the necessary papers. On June 25, 1959, the copyright on *Betty Boop* was renewed in Max's name.

Thanks to Stanley Handman's watchful eye, Betty Boop stayed where she belonged: in the loving hands of her creator, Max Fleischer.

When Fleischer Studios first started to investigate the possibility of reintroducing Betty Boop to the public, it was quite surprised to find how recognizable and how loved she still was. Her popularity was not much diminished from her heyday in the 1930s and 1940s.

There were offers from various companies to "do something" with the character, like creating a new television series or mounting a Broadway musical. However, for one reason or another, all the proposed deals collapsed.

Meanwhile, time was not being kind to Max. He never fully

accepted the reality that his case against Paramount was over, so he kept researching legal books and dictating more memos to Vera. It was a sign that changes, cruel changes, were taking place inside his head.

Max never left the apartment except to go to one of his doctors. Slowly he began to withdraw within himself. He was speaking less and less. That brilliant, creative, inventive mind was slowing down. With what he had been through, it was a wonder that it had lasted as long as it had.

Essie, my mother, was always much more extroverted than Max and given to short bursts of furious temper. A kind of cabin fever was developing. She loved being outdoors, traveling, going places, playing poker with her friends.

Now she was all but locked in, taking care of her husband, staring out the windows, looking at the hard, concrete canyons of Manhattan instead of the grounds and gardens of her beloved Miami Beach home. Eventually, she began to talk of suicide, of jumping out one of the windows of their eleventh-floor apartment. She would frighten my sister, Ruth, with hysterical phone calls that, day or night, would bring Ruth in a panic from the other side of town.

It was becoming more and more apparent that a retirement home would be the next step. And then the Motion Picture Country House came into our lives.

From the time I started directing movies in Hollywood in 1945, I'd heard about the Motion Picture Country House (MPCH). A small percentage of my salary was automatically deducted and donated to it. Almost everyone in the picture business did the same. I knew it was a retirement home meant exclusively for people who worked in the industry in any capacity. It didn't matter whether you had money; if you were eligible, you would be accepted. Although I'd supported the MPCH, I'd never visited it or even seen it. That changed dramatically when a location survey for a film I was preparing took me to the San Fernando Valley and the MPCH.

It looked like a cover from *House and Garden* magazine. Immaculately kept grounds, charming small cottages, a bright and cheerful dining room, a first-run, state-of-the-art movie theater, a medical wing where every room had its own private garden. Nothing was spared to make this place an inviting, beautiful, first-class facility. It lifted your heart just being there.

I knew that this was the place for my parents, and I immediately started the process to get them admitted. When I phoned Ruth in New York and told her about it, she all but passed out from sheer happiness. And apparently so did my mother when Ruth told her about it. However, it was my father who balked. He had too much work to do. He needed an office. He needed a secretary. He needed his research books and papers.

It wasn't long before the MPCH admitted Max and Essie. When I thanked the admittance board, their reply was: "This is exactly why the MPCH was created. Particularly for famous movie people who need financial help."

Max was really being very stubborn. He was adamant about not going, and there was no way we could or would force him. Finally, I flew to New York armed with brochures, pictures, and literature and pitched him a real hard sell. I was able to answer all his objections. About having an office, I pointed out to him that I had requested two side-by-side cottages so that he could use one as an office and sleep there as well, just as he did at home, where he had taken to using his office as a bedroom. I guaranteed that I'd have all his books and papers shipped to him. As far as a secretary was concerned, I had talked it over with Vera and offered her a small salary and all expenses if she would come to California and continue to take dictation. She leaped at the suggestion. Just like my parents, she couldn't stand the winters in New York.

Max ran out of objections and grudgingly gave in. I returned to Los Angeles and awaited the arrival of Max, Essie, Vera, and Ruth, who would chaperone them. In mid-1967, Max and Essie checked into the MPCH.

Everything worked out perfectly. Essie was in heaven with her plantings around the cottages as well as her crossword puzzles, to both of which she was fanatically dedicated. We found a small apartment for Vera in a motel not far from the MPCH. There was a city bus that took her right to the entrance. And Max snored contentedly all through his "dictation" sessions.

Mickey, my wonderful wife, and I settled into a comfortable routine for visiting. Every Sunday we would pick up Vera in our car, then collect the folks and have lunch at a nearby Hamburger Hamlet. We missed very few of those Sunday visits in all the years Max and Essie remained at the MPCH.

As pleasant as everything was at the MPCH, the years were taking their toll on Max. His mind was doing a long fade-out. One of the most annoying things for Essie was his knocking on her cottage door at three or four in the morning. She'd open the door, and there he'd be completely dressed with shoes, shirt, tie, slacks, jacket, and fedora hat. He was ready to go, but he didn't know where. Essie would—not too graciously—take him back to his cottage, undress him, and put him back to bed. It was like putting a child to sleep and was still part of the reverse life cycle that he seemed to be following.

And even further back in this cycle was the fact that, after a while, he stopped speaking altogether. It was as though, like an infant, he had not yet learned how.

28

The year 1972 turned out to be a most significant one for everyone connected with the Max Fleischer story. It started with two very bright young ladies who worked in New York for King Features Syndicate, one of the largest merchandise-licensing companies in the world. It was the same King Features that had licensed *Popeye the Sailor* to Fleischer Studios in the 1930s.

In going through some files, the young ladies came across Popeye's first animated cartoon appearance, his screen test really—the *Betty Boop* cartoon *Popeye the Sailor.* It struck the two girls that Betty hadn't been seen in a long time and that she seemed like a natural for merchandising. They decided that they would try to develop Betty Boop into a sellable product.

They turned their idea over to the company's director of radio and special services, John H. Wright, to try to track down the character's present owner. Wright located Ruth, who lived in New York, and she turned him over to me and our lawyer,

Stanley Handman. Fleischer Studios signed a contract with King Features on August 1, 1972.

Another significant thing happened in 1972. Max died.

On Sunday, September 10, Mickey and I were, as usual, at the Motion Picture Country House. We had picked up Vera and were now walking with Essie to the hospital to visit my father. He'd taken a fall two weeks earlier and had injured his left leg. In spite of all that the splendid hospital staff could do, the leg had turned gangrenous. When we visited the previous week, he was semiconscious. I'm not sure he knew we were there.

Now, when we walked into the room, my stomach turned. Max had deteriorated terribly. He seemed unconscious except that his left hand kept plucking at the blanket covering the infected leg. He seemed to be in some pain.

My mother quietly told Mickey and me that the doctors wanted to amputate but that she wouldn't give them her permission. "He's going to die soon," she had told them, "and I don't want him mutilated." Then she said: "I can't stand watching him like this. Let's go have some lunch. I've got to get away from here."

Essie walked to the side of the bed away from the leg, then leaned over to get her mouth close to his ear, steadying herself with her arm propped against the mattress. "Max," she said loudly into his ear. "We're going now, but we'll be back soon."

Suddenly my father grabbed Essie's wrist with his right hand. It startled us all a bit. She tried to pull her hand away, but he hung on. "Max, let go," she said, struggling against his grip, but he hung on to her. My mother seemed a little panicky. She looked at us with surprise. "He won't let go! I didn't know he was that strong!" With her other hand, she grabbed at his fingers, trying to pry them off her wrist. "Come here, and help me," she yelled, trying even harder to break loose. I was just about there when she got her wrist free and hustled out of the room.

I was heartbroken by that little drama. I felt that my father knew that he was dying and didn't want to be left alone. He was afraid. He wanted Essie close to him.

My father passed away early the next morning. He was eighty-nine years old.

The terrible irony of the whole thing was that he died eleven days after the signing of the King Features contract. He never saw Fleischer Studios blossom into a multimillion-dollar company or got to enjoy the bright and shining newfound success of his creation, Betty Boop.

Index

and army training films, 26–27, 40, 125; and Betty Boop, creation, 50–52; and Betty Boop, end of, 103–4; and Betty Boop lawsuit, 56–57; and "bouncing ball" for lyrics on films, 37, 43, 48; at Bray Studios, 24–30; with *Brooklyn Daily Eagle,* 7–8, 9–11; at Crouse-Hinds Company, 11–12; and Dave, relationship strain, 107–11, 119, 148–49; and Famous Studios, loss of papers from, 127–29, 134; financial troubles, 1960s, 154, 155–61; and Fleischer Studios, beginnings, 47–48; and Fleischer Studios, environment, 87–89; and Fleischer Studios, Union troubles, 89–92; and Great Depression, success during, 59–61; *Gulliver's Travels,* 97, 101–3, 104, 107, 109, 149; at Jam Handy Organization, 125–30, 131–32, 156; machines, interest in, 11–12, 13, 14, 15; and Miami move, 94–96; and music/musicians for cartoons, 33, 49, 109–10, 120; and new copyright law, 163–

64; and outdoor movie theater, 13–14; Out of the Inkwell companies, 32–38, 45–47, 153; and Paramount, 1929 contract, 48, 50; and Paramount, 1938 financial support agreement for Miami move, 96, 115, 149–50; and Paramount, 1941 contract, 113–17, 122, 148–50, 151; and Paramount, cartoon ownership, 48, 116, 133–35, 145; and Paramount, lawsuit against, 141–46, 147–50, 151, 153–54, 156; and Paramount, patent ownerships, 122, 145; and Paramount, resignation from, 120–21; and Paramount, royalty checks for cartoons, 121–22, 157–61; *Popeye,* ix, 53–55, 85, 156; at *Popular Science Monthly,* 12, 13–17; and Red Seal Pictures distribution company, 45–46, 50; and Rialto movie theater, 40–44; *Rudolph the Red Nosed Reindeer,* 130, 141; *Screen Songs,* 50, 51, 151, 156, 157–58; *Song Car-Tunes,* 37–38, 43–44, 48, 50; *Superman* cartoons, ix, 104–5, 116,

45, 154; Ko-Ko the Clown revived for, 151–53; Paramount sale of Fleischer cartoons to, 133–34, 144, 163; reediting of cartoons for, 134–35, 142, 144

Twenty Thousand Leagues under the Sea (movie) (R. Fleischer), 132, 137–38

Vallee, Rudy, 51
Vanishing American, The (movie), 41
Variety, 136, 153
Vernick, Edith, 87
Video House, 152–53

Wagner Labor Relations Act (1935), 90

Waldman, Myron, 52
Walker, Card, 137
Walsh, Bill, 137
Warner Brothers, 144
Weiss, Alfred, 46–47, 48, 50
Welling, N. William, 110, 115
West, Mae, 103
Windermere Hotel apartment (11J), 61, 63–68, 92, 131, 142, 155; and television-watching for lawsuit, 143–44
Winkler, Margaret, 32
World War I, 26–27
World War II, 120, 125
Wright, John H., 169

Xerox Corporation, 102

Zukor, Adolph, 24, 83, 94, 134

CPSIA information can be obtained
at www.ICGtesting.com
Printed in the USA
BVOW03s2331111117
500198BV00001B/9/P